FIRST 50 BROADWAY SONGS
YOU SHOULD SING

Andrew Lloyd Webber™ is a trademark owned by Andrew Lloyd Webber.

ISBN 978-1-4950-7461-5

HAL•LEONARD®

7777 W. BLUEMOUND RD. P.O. BOX 13819 MILWAUKEE, WI 53213

Visit Hal Leonard Online at
www.halleonard.com

CONTENTS

ANY DREAM WILL DO

from JOSEPH AND THE AMAZING TECHNICOLOR® DREAMCOAT

Music by ANDREW LLOYD WEBBER
Lyrics by TIM RICE

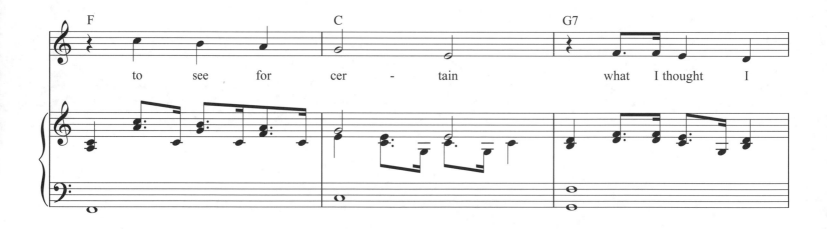

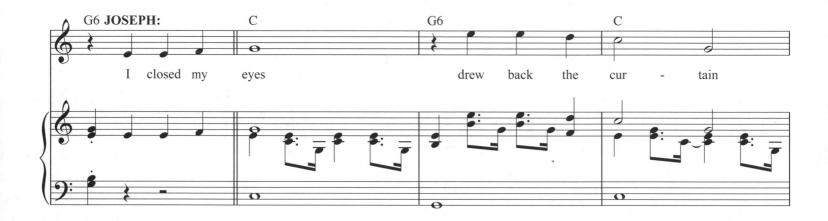

weep - ing, but the world was sleep - ing,

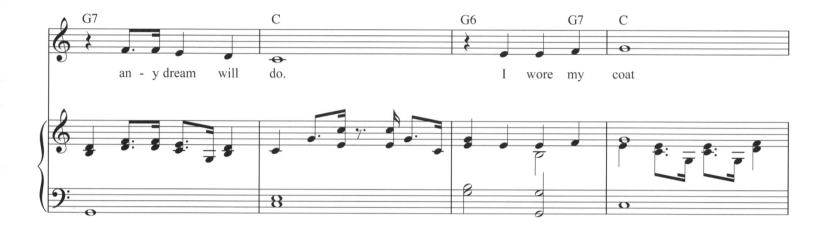

an - y dream will do. I wore my coat

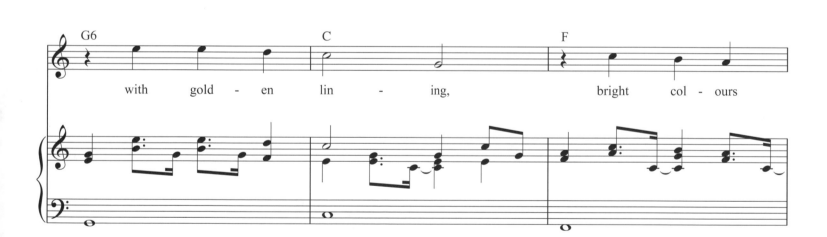

with gold - en lin - ing, bright col - ours

shin - ing won - der - ful and new.

And in the east the dawn was break - ing,

and the world was wak - ing, an - y dream will

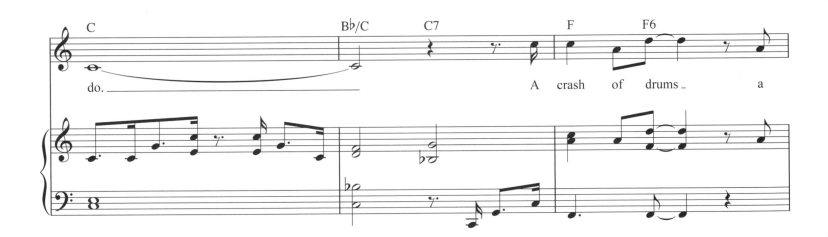

do. _____ A crash of drums _ a

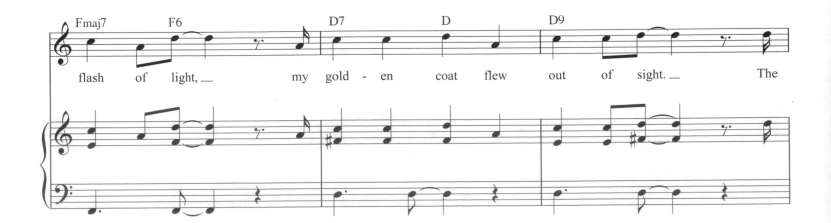

flash of light, _ my gold - en coat flew out of sight. _ The

col - ours fad - ed in - to dark - ness, I was left a - lone. _____

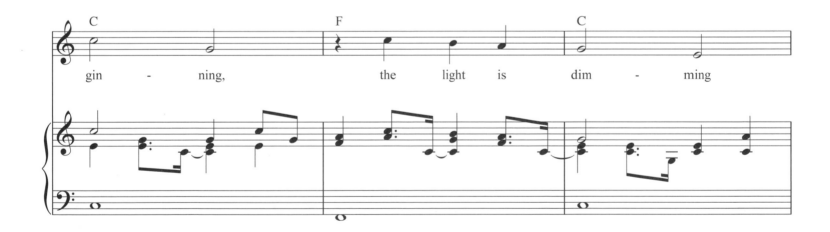

_____ May I re - turn, to the be -

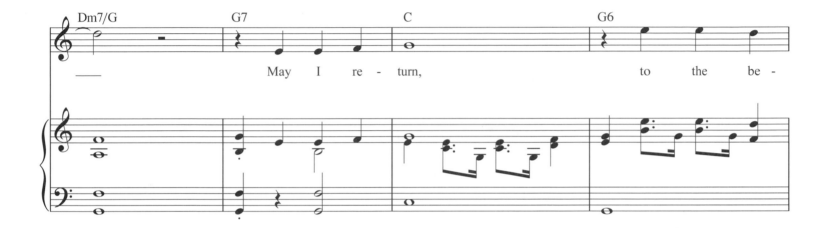

gin - ning, the light is dim - ming

and the dream is too, the world and I,

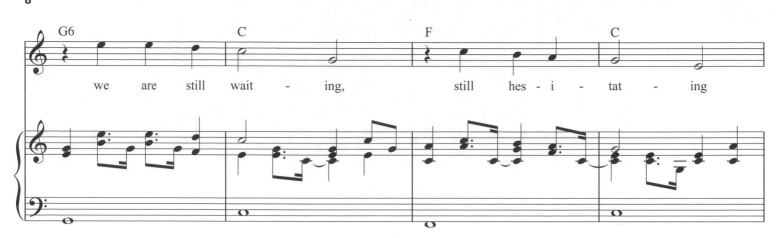

we are still wait - ing, still hes - i - tat - ing

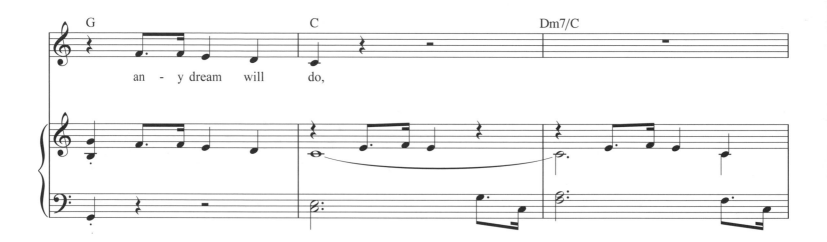

an - y dream will do,

an - y dream will do,

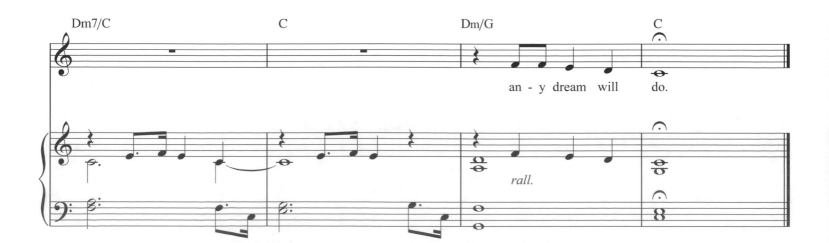

an - y dream will do.

rall.

ANYTHING GOES
from ANYTHING GOES

Words and Music by
COLE PORTER

Moderately

In old-en days, a glimpse of stock-ing was

looked on as some-thing shock - ing, now, heav-en knows, _____

_____ an-y-thing goes. _____ Good au-thors, too, who

once knew bet - ter words now on - ly use four - let - ter words writ - ing

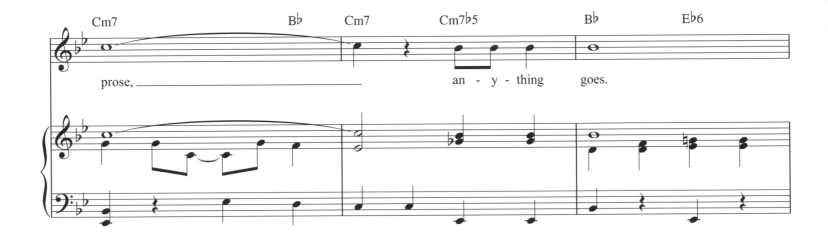

prose, _____ an - y - thing goes.

The world has gone mad to - day, __ and good's bad to - day, __ and black's

white to - day, __ and day's night to - day, __ when most guys to - day __ that wom - en

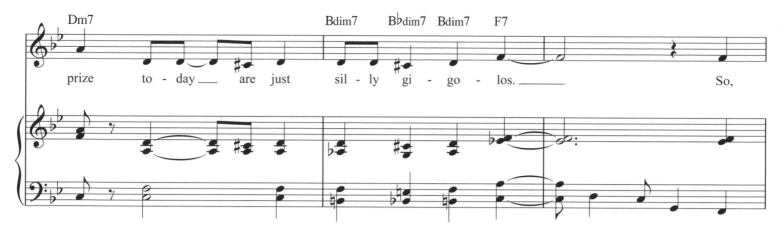

prize to - day ___ are just sil - ly gi - go - los. ___ So,

though I'm not a great ro - manc - er, I know that {you're / I'm} bound to an -

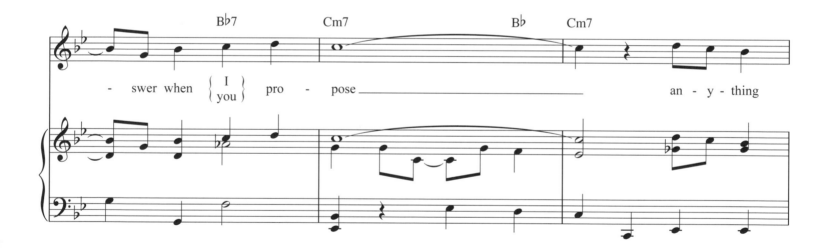

- swer when {I / you} pro - pose ___ an - y - thing

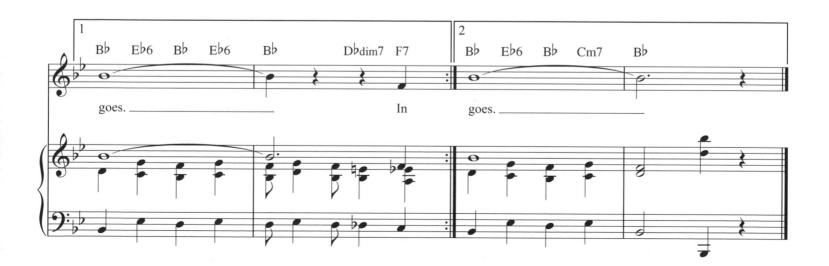

goes. ___   In   goes. ___

AS LONG AS HE NEEDS ME

from the Broadway Musical OLIVER!

Words and Music by
LIONEL BART

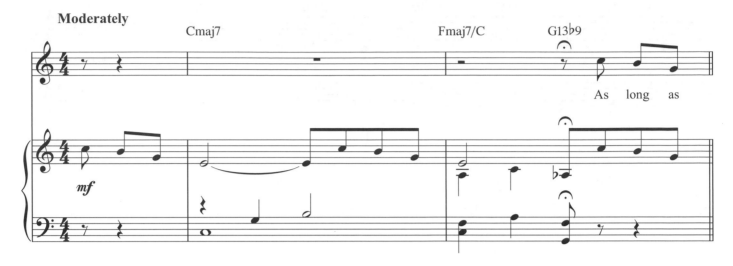

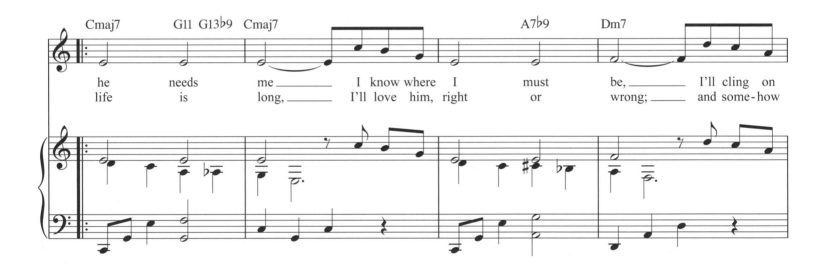

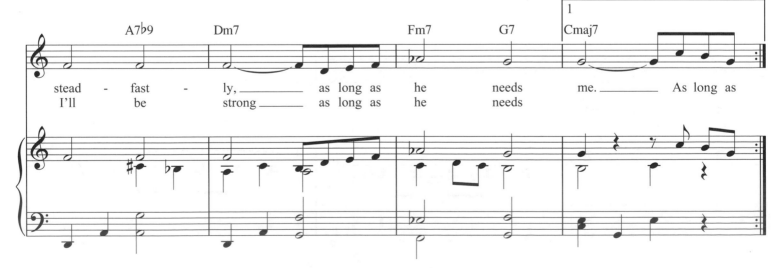

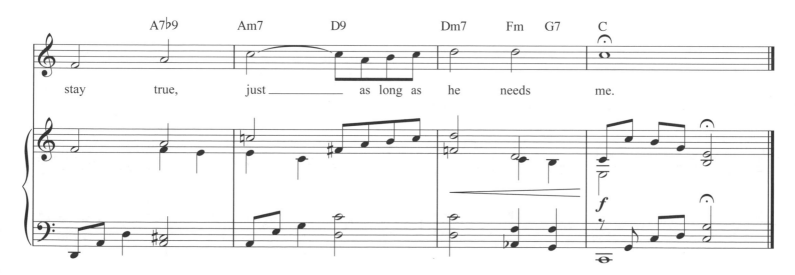

BEAUTY AND THE BEAST

from BEAUTY AND THE BEAST: THE BROADWAY MUSICAL

Music by ALAN MENKEN
Lyrics by HOWARD ASHMAN

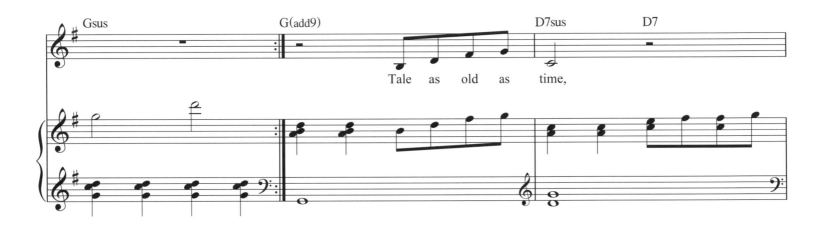

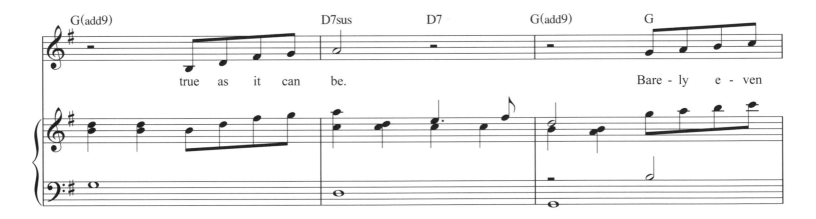

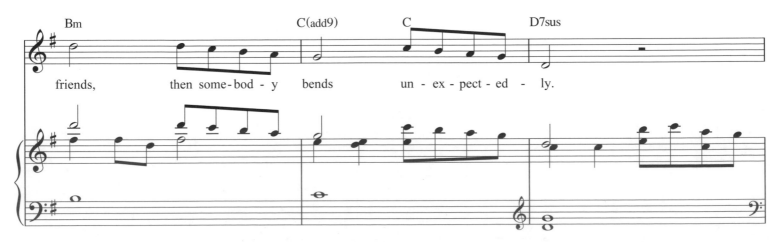

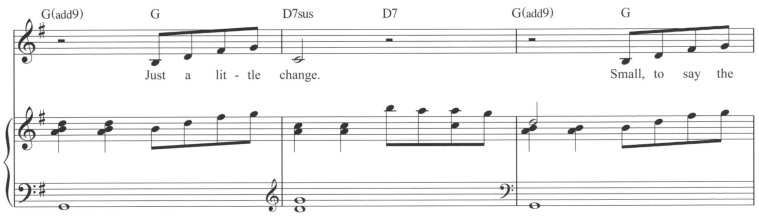

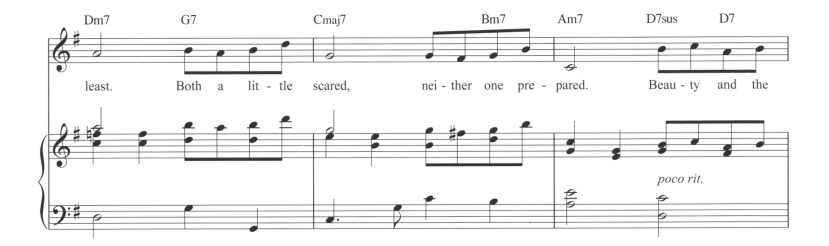

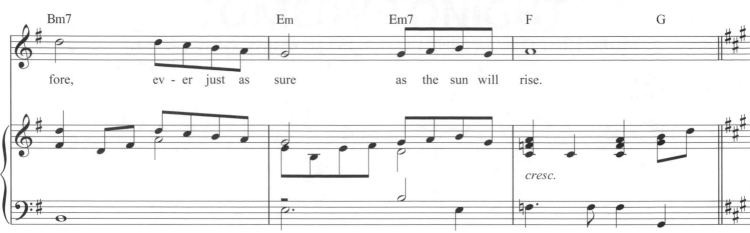

fore, ev - er just as sure as the sun will rise.

Tale as old as time. Tune as old as

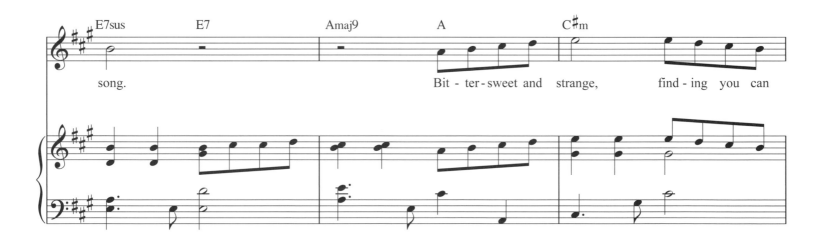

song. Bit - ter - sweet and strange, find - ing you can

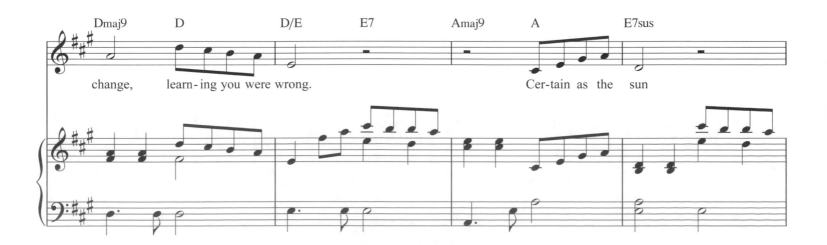

change, learn - ing you were wrong. Cer - tain as the sun

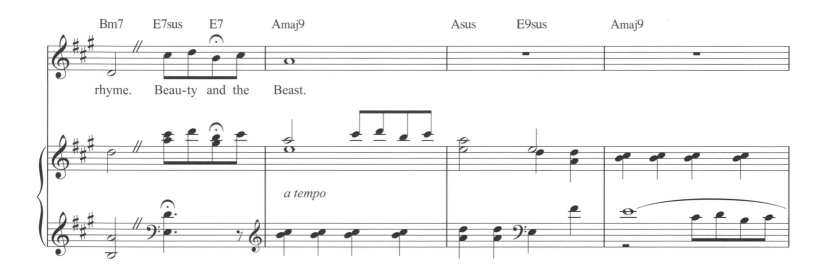

BROADWAY BABY

from FOLLIES

Music and Lyrics by
STEPHEN SONDHEIM

- kl-ing lights, _ A spark _ To pierce the _ dark ____ From Bat - t'ry _ Park _

____ To _ Wash - ing-ton Heights! _ Some - day, may - be, ____

_ All my dreams will be re - paid. __

Hell, I'd ev - en play the _ maid ____ To be in a show. ____

Say, ___ Mis - ter Pro - du - cer, ___

I'm ___ talk - ing to you, ___ sir: ___ I don't need a lot,

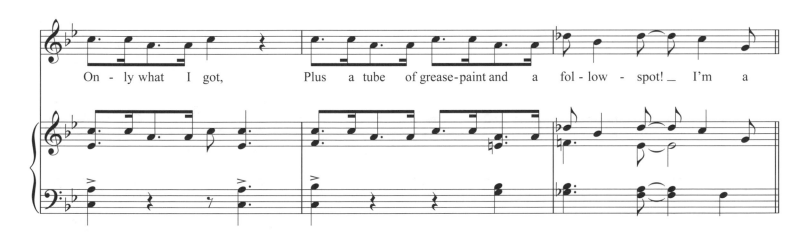

On - ly what I got, Plus a tube of grease-paint and a fol - low - spot! ___ I'm a

Broad - way ba - by, ___ Slav - ing at a five - and - ten, ___

Dream - ing of the great day when _____ I'll be in a

show. _____

Broad - way ba - by, _____ Mak - ing rounds all af - ter - noon, ___

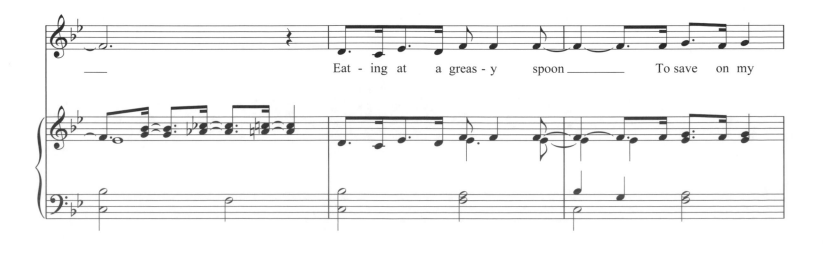

Eat - ing at a greas - y spoon _____ To save on my

dough.

At ___ My ti - ny ___ flat ___ There's just my __ cat, _____ A ___ bed __

___ and a chair. __ Still, ___ I'll stick it ___ till _____ I'm on a ___ bill __

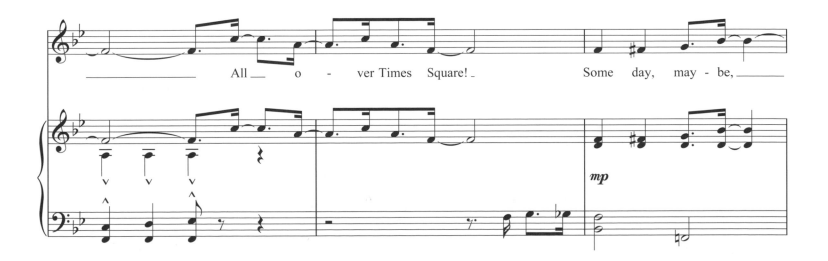

_____ All __ o - ver Times Square! _ Some day, may - be, _____

24

CAN'T HELP LOVIN' DAT MAN

from SHOW BOAT

Lyrics by OSCAR HAMMERSTEIN II
Music by JEROME KERN

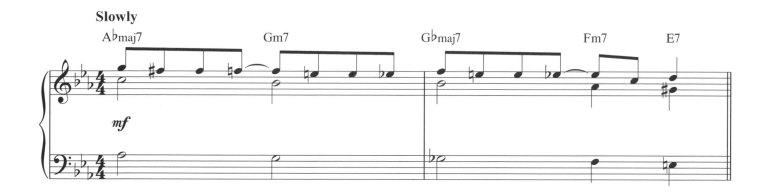

Slowly

Fish got to swim _ and birds got to fly, _ I got to love _ one
Tell me he's la - zy, tell me he's slow, _ tell me I'm cra - zy,

man till I die. _ } Can't help lov - in' dat man _ of
may - be I know. _ }

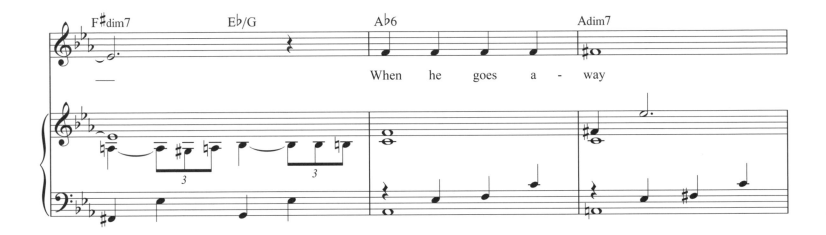

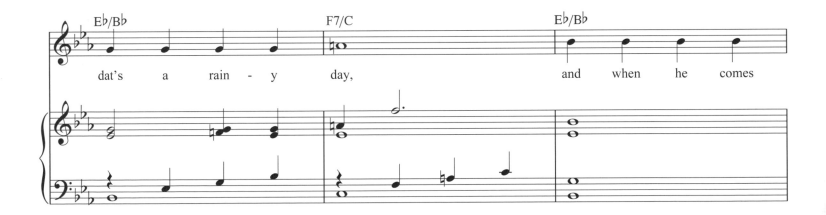

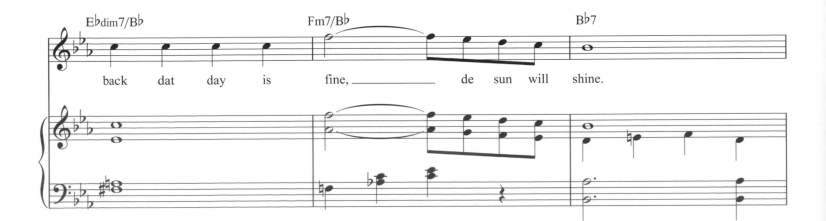

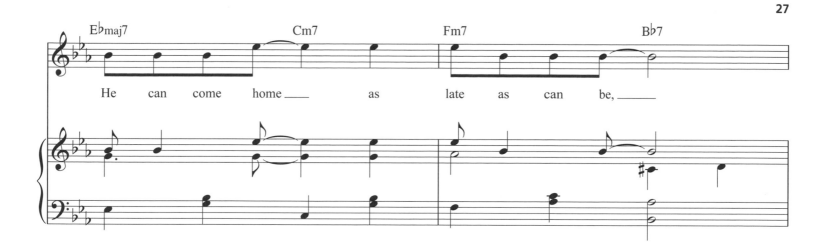

He can come home _____ as late as can be, _____

home wid - out him _____ ain't no home to me. _____

To Coda ⊕

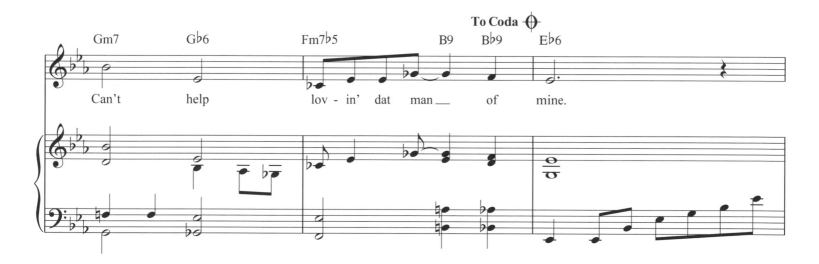

Can't help lov - in' dat man _____ of mine.

D.S. al Coda
(take repeat)

CODA ⊕

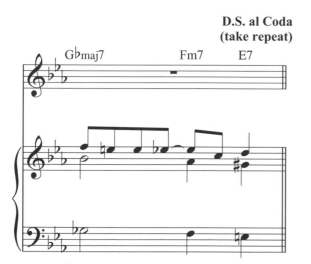

mine. _____

CABARET
from the Musical CABARET

Words by FRED EBB
Music by JOHN KANDER

Moderately

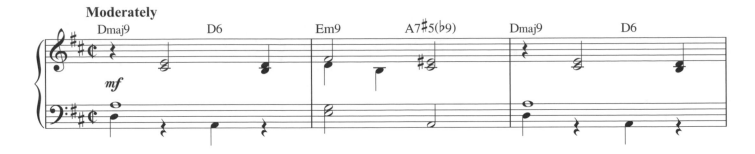

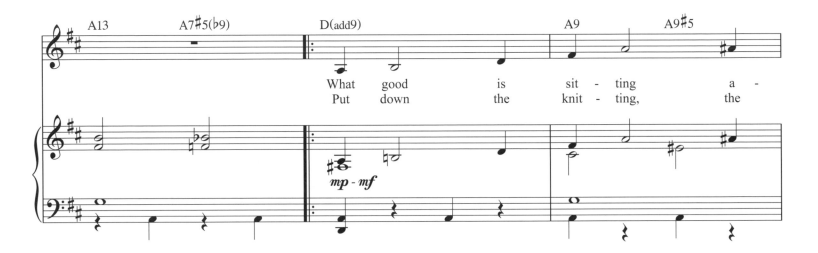

What good is sit- ting a-
Put down the knit- ting, the

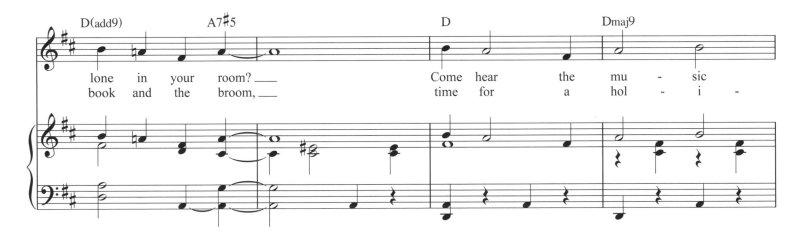

lone in your room? ___ Come hear the mu - sic
book and the broom, ___ time for a hol - i -

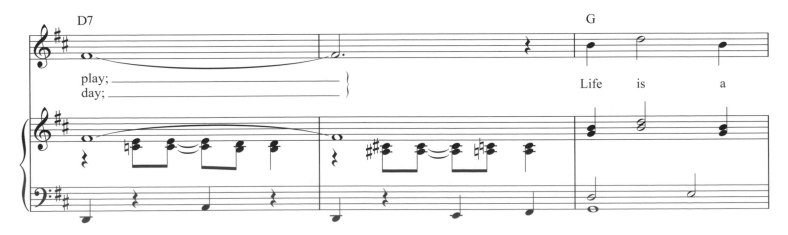

play; ___
day; ___

Life is a

30

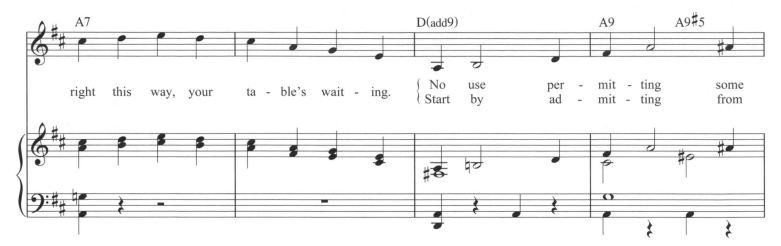

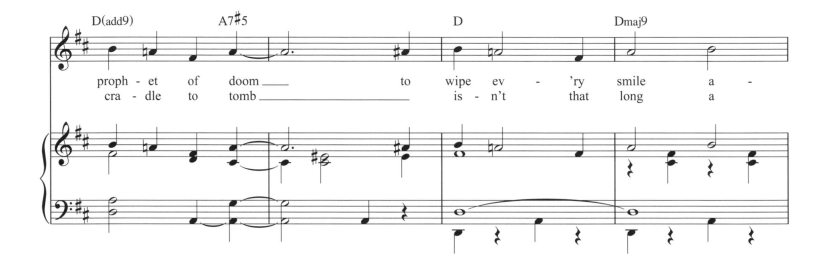

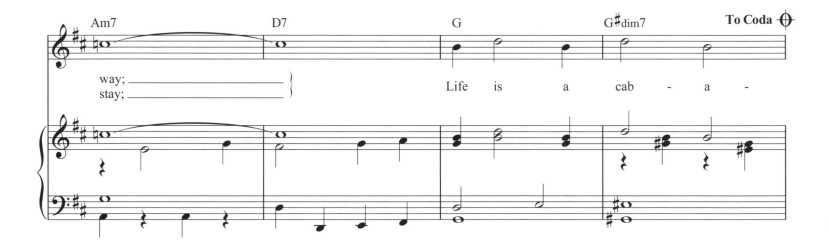

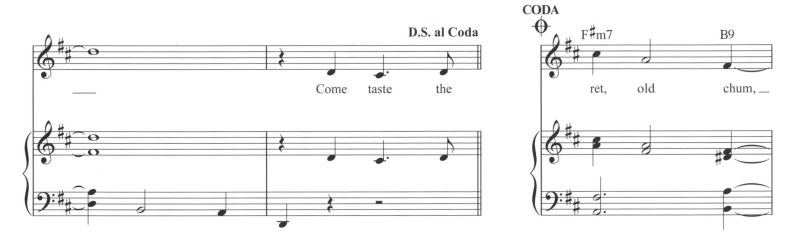

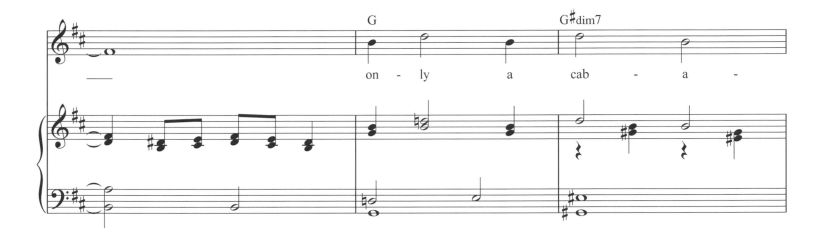

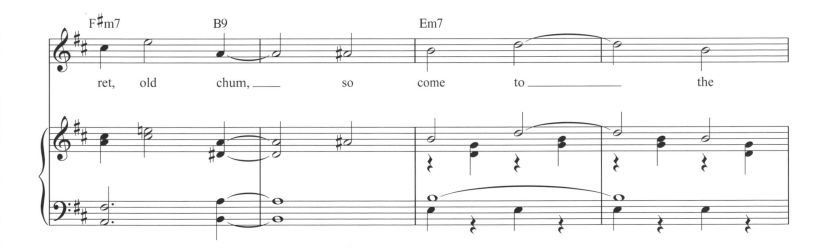

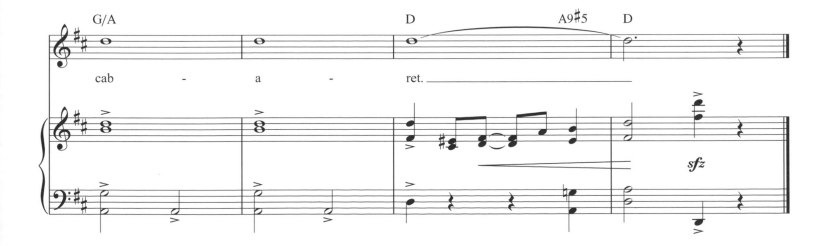

COMEDY TONIGHT
from A FUNNY THING HAPPENED ON THE WAY TO THE FORUM

Music and Lyrics by
STEPHEN SONDHEIM

Brightly

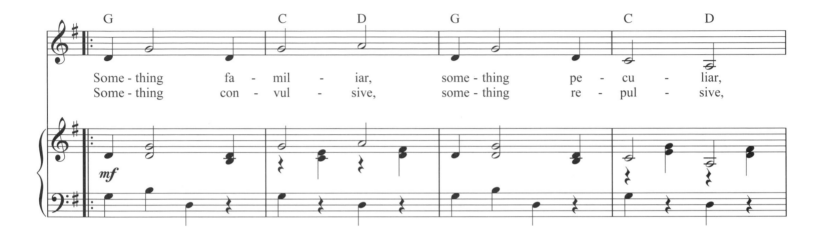

Some - thing fa - mil - iar, some - thing pe - cu - liar,
Some - thing con - vul - sive, some - thing re - pul - sive,

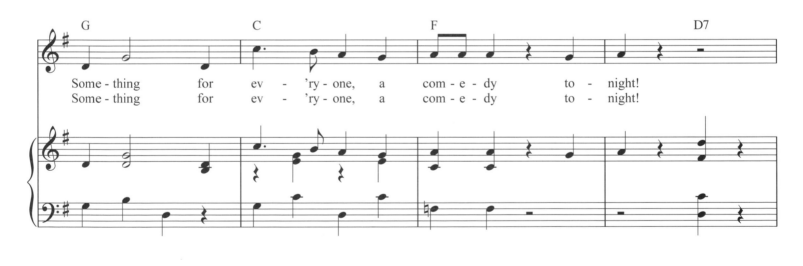

Some - thing for ev - 'ry - one, a com - e - dy to - night!
Some - thing for ev - 'ry - one, a com - e - dy to - night!

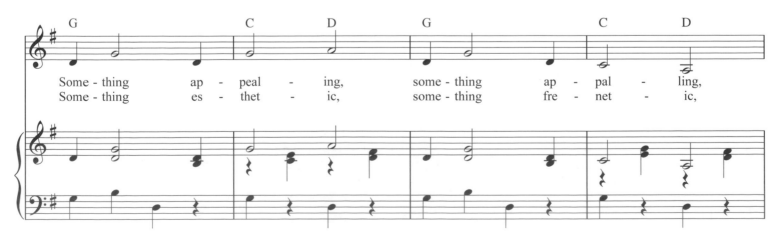

Some - thing ap - peal - ing, some - thing ap - pal - ling,
Some - thing es - thet - ic, some - thing fre - net - ic,

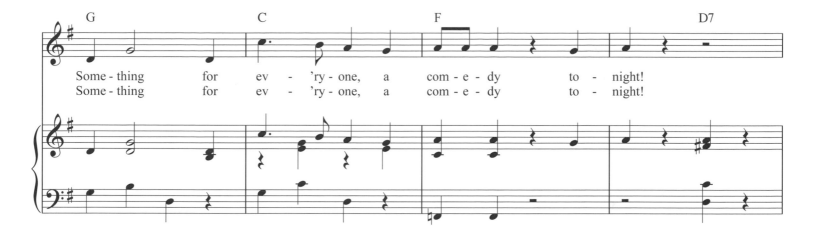

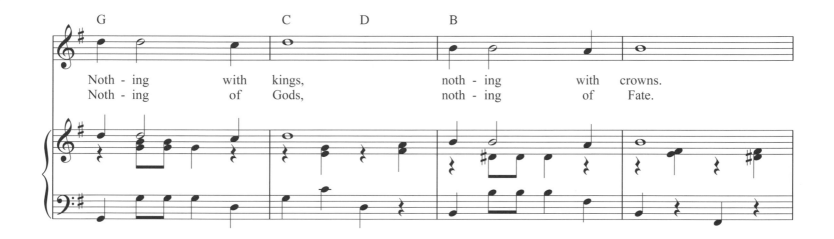

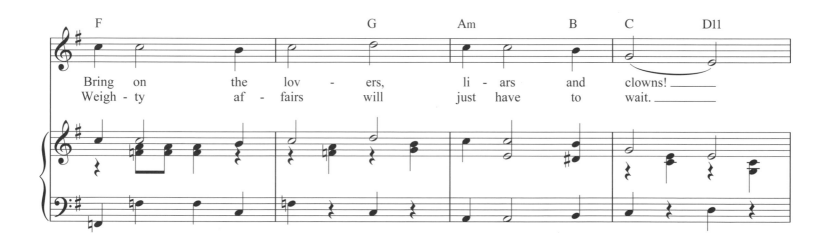

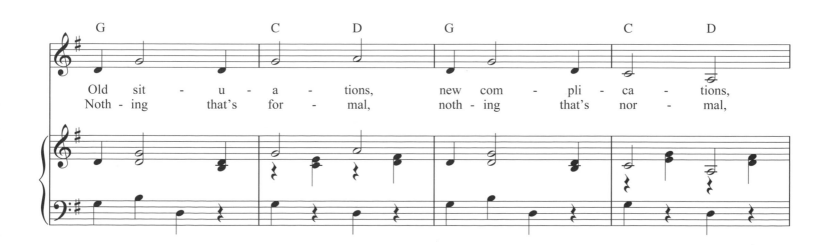

Nothing por - ten - tous or po - lite; _____
No re - ci - ta - tions to re - cite! _____

Trag - e - dy to - mor - row, com - e - dy to - night!
O - pen up the cur - tain,

com - e - dy _____

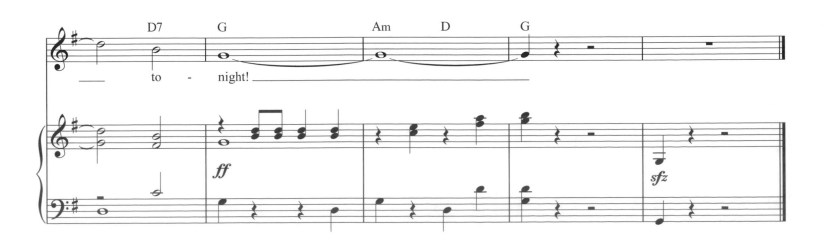

_____ to - night! _____

EDELWEISS
from THE SOUND OF MUSIC

Lyrics by OSCAR HAMMERSTEIN II
Music by RICHARD RODGERS

Moderato

Refrain *(slowly, with expression)*

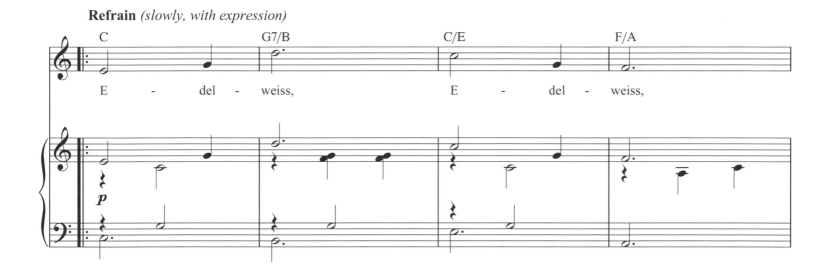

E - del - weiss, E - del - weiss,

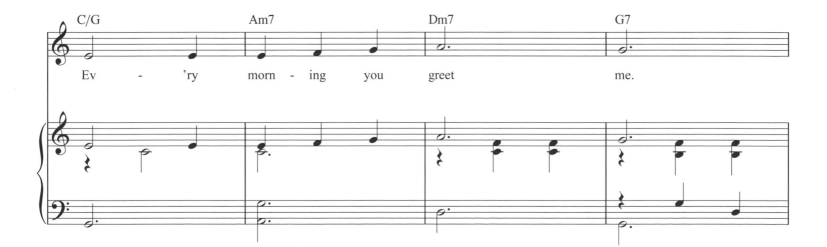

Ev - 'ry morn - ing you greet me.

Small and white, Clean and bright,

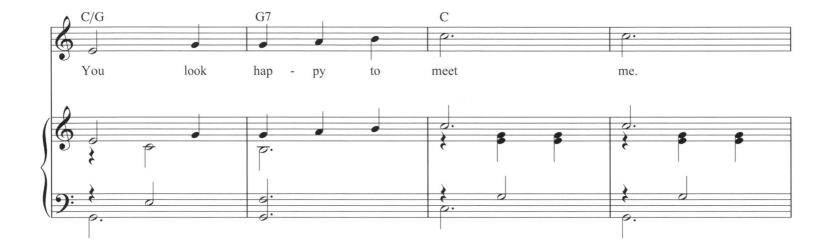

You look hap - py to meet me.

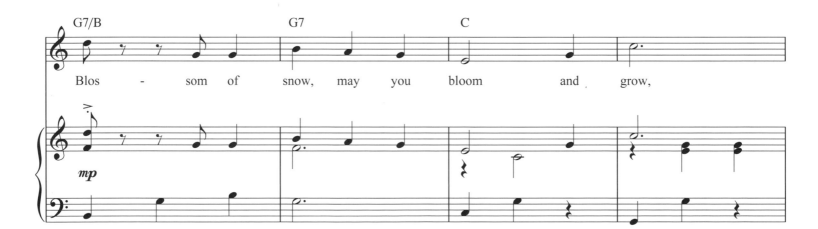

Blos - som of snow, may you bloom and grow,

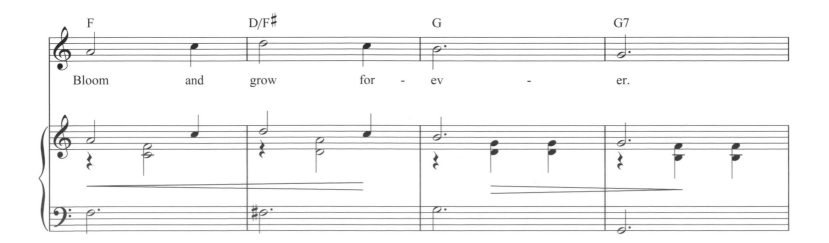

Bloom and grow for - ev - er.

DON'T CRY FOR ME ARGENTINA

from EVITA

Words by TIM RICE
Music by ANDREW LLOYD WEBBER

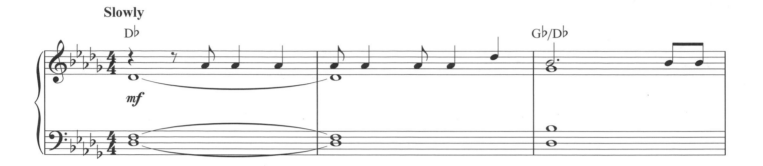

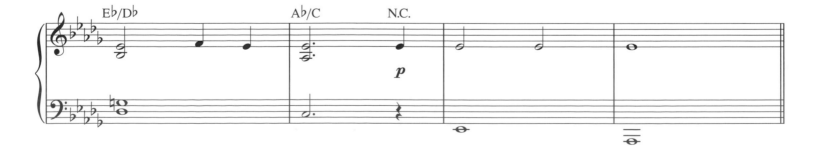

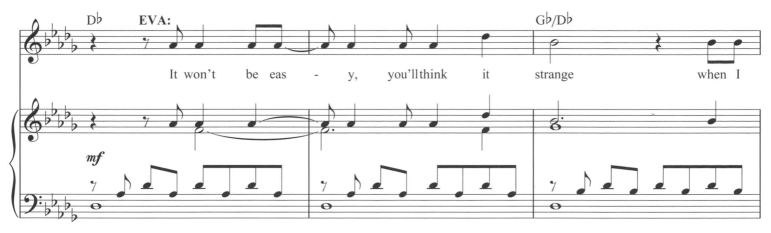

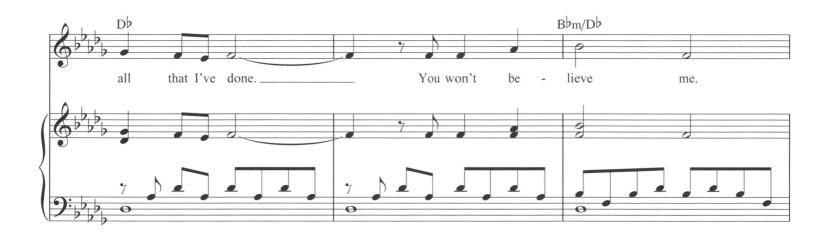

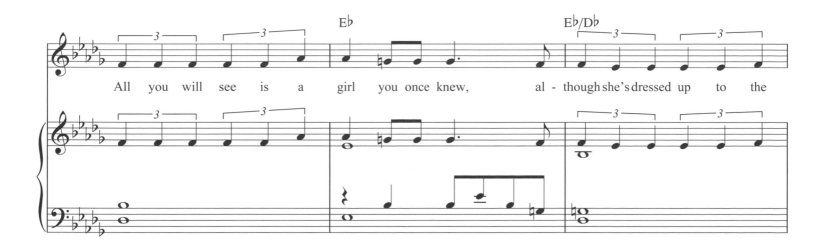

nines, at six - es and sev - ens with you.

I had to let it hap - pen, I had to change, could - n't spend all my life down at

heel, look - ing out of the win - dow, stay - ing out of the sun. So I chose

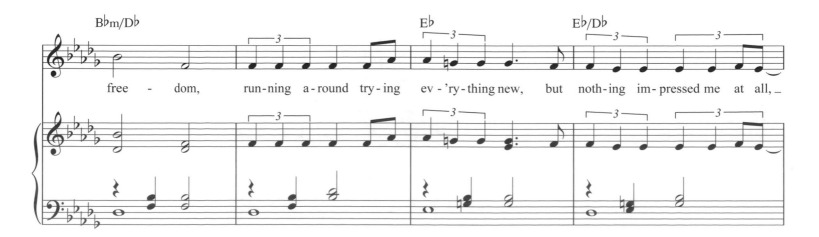

free - dom, run - ning a - round try - ing ev - 'ry - thing new, but noth - ing im - pressed me at all, _

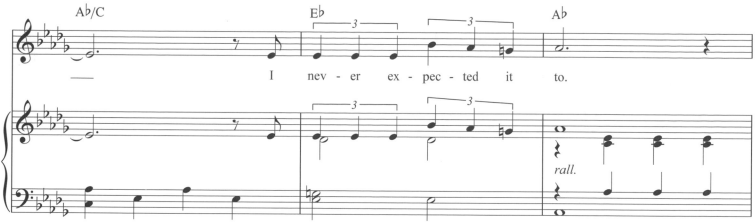

I nev - er ex - pec - ted it to.

Don't cry for me Ar - gen - ti - na, _____ the truth is I nev - er

left you. All through my wild days, _____ my mad ex - is - tence, _____ I kept my

prom - ise, don't keep your dis - tance. _____

And as for for - tune and as for fame, I

nev - er in - vit - ed them in, though it seemed to the world _ they were

all I de - sired. They are il - lu - sions, they're

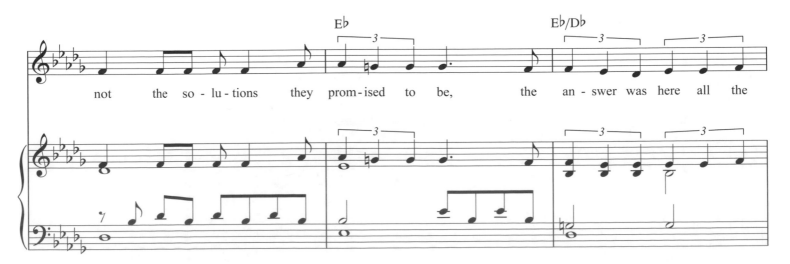

not the so - lu - tions they prom - ised to be, the an - swer was here all the

time, I love you and hope you love me.

Don't cry for me Ar - gen - ti - na.   Mm _____

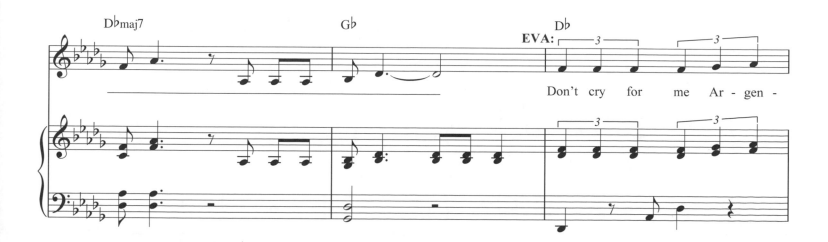

Don't cry for me Ar - gen -

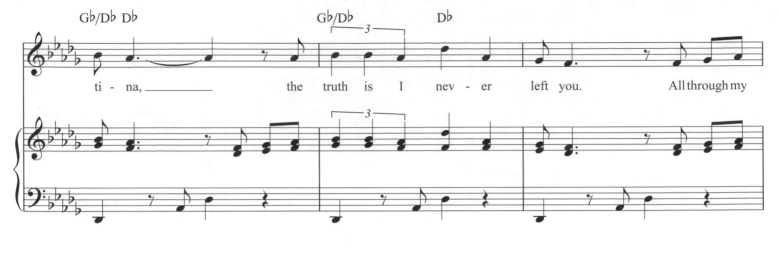

ti - na, _____ the truth is I nev - er left you. All through my

wild days, _____ my mad ex - is - tence, I kept my prom - ise, don't keep your

dis - tance. _____ Have I said too much, there's noth - ing more I can think of to

say to you. ___ But all you have to do is

look at me to know that ev - 'ry word is true. ___

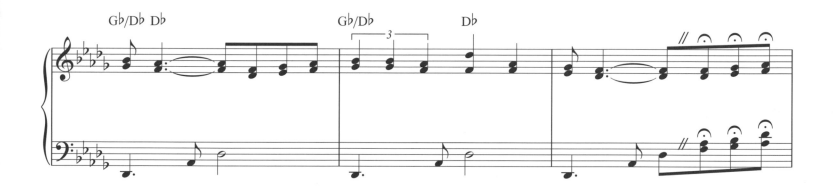

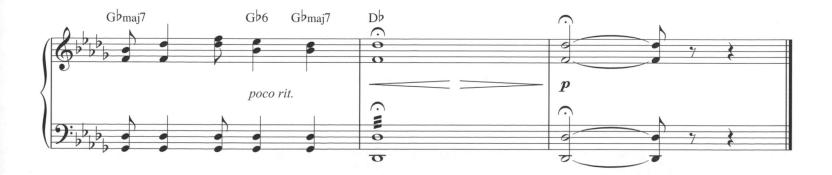

EVERYTHING'S COMING UP ROSES

from GYPSY

Lyrics by STEPHEN SONDHEIM
Music by JULE STYNE

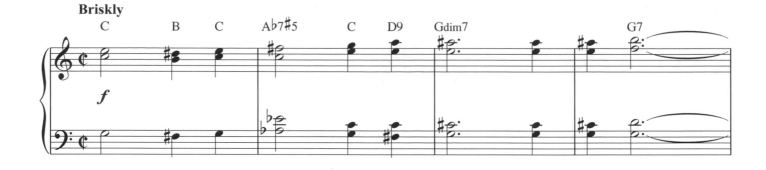

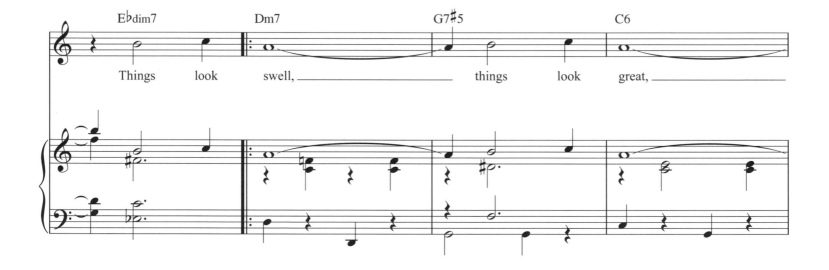

Things look swell, _____ things look great, _____

_____ gon - na have the whole world _____ on a plate. _____

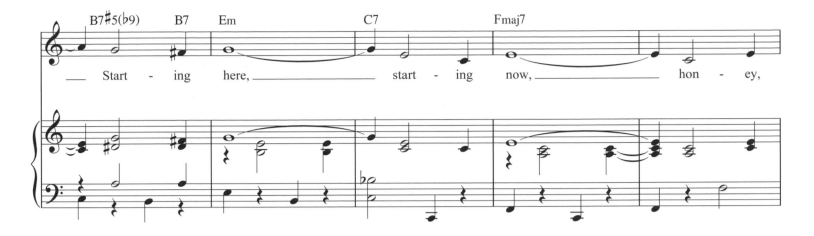

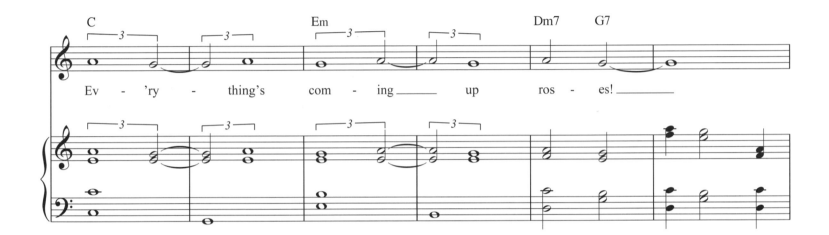

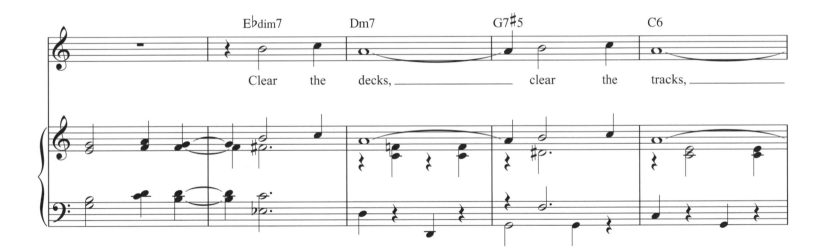

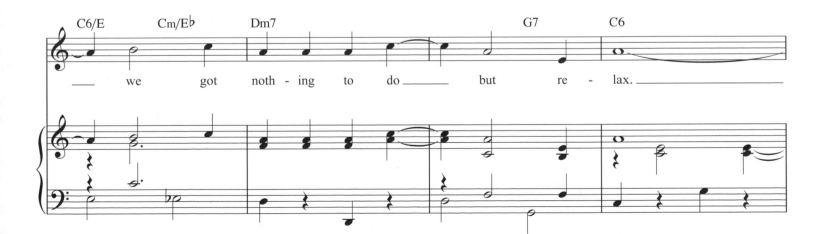

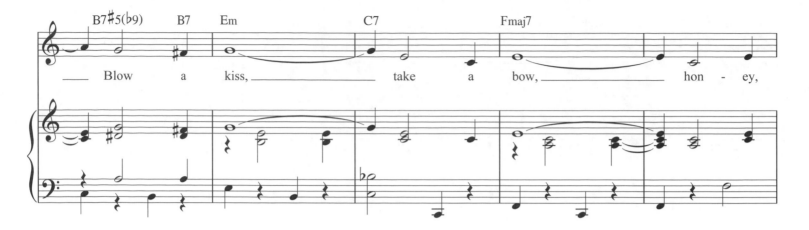

Blow a kiss, _____ take a bow, _____ hon - ey,

Ev - 'ry - thing's com - ing _____ up ros - es! _____

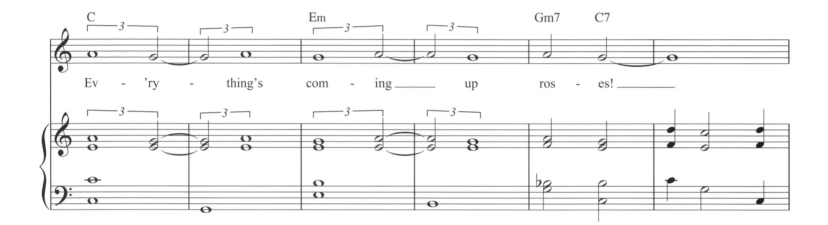

Now's our _____

in - ning, _____ stand the world on its ear! ___

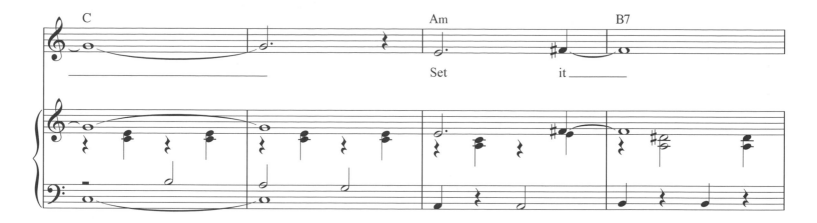

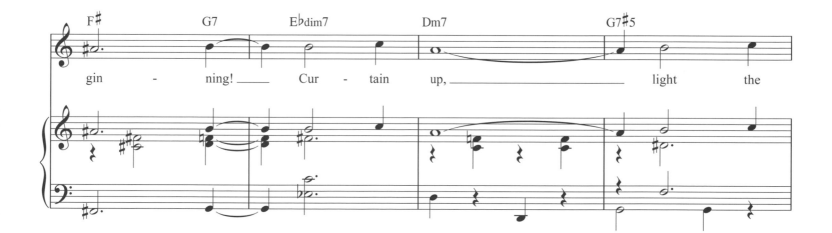

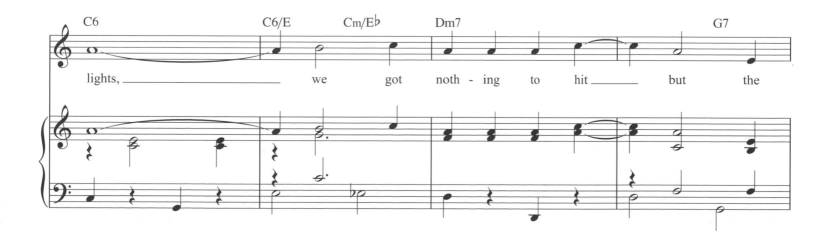

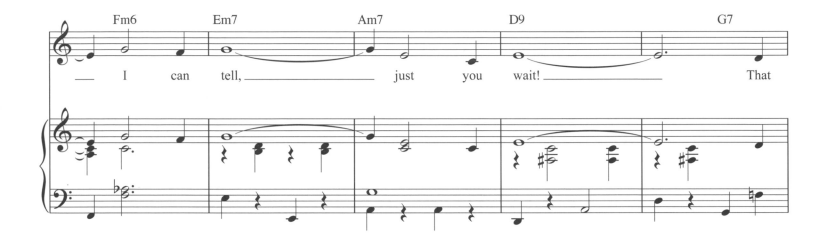

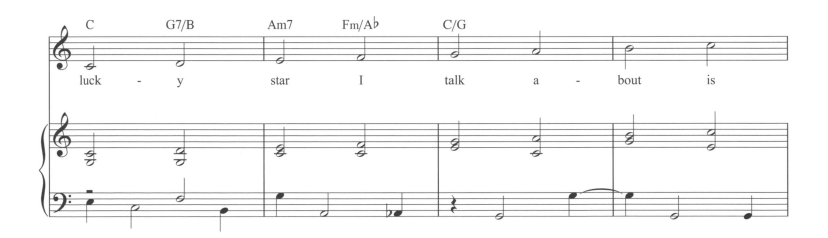

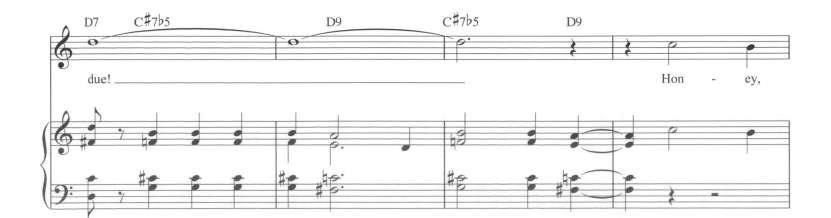

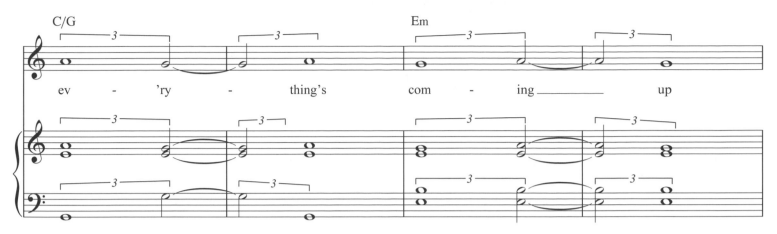

ev - 'ry - thing's com - ing _____ up

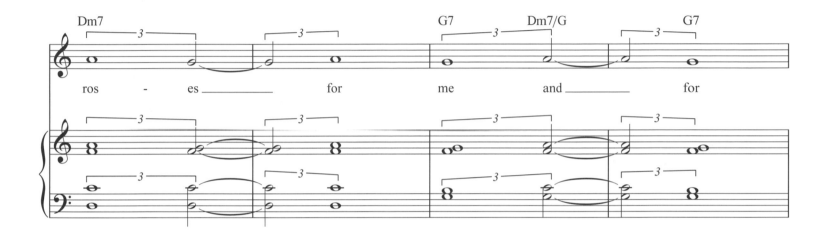

ros - es _____ for me and _____ for

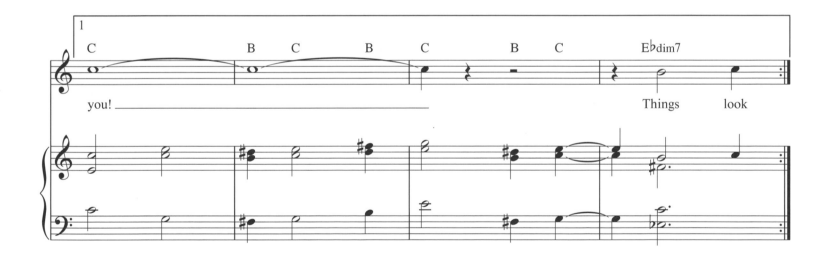

you! _____ Things look

you! _____

FOR GOOD
from the Broadway Musical WICKED

Music and Lyrics by
STEPHEN SCHWARTZ

Note: When performed as a solo, sing the top melody line throughout.

Tenderly, poco rubato

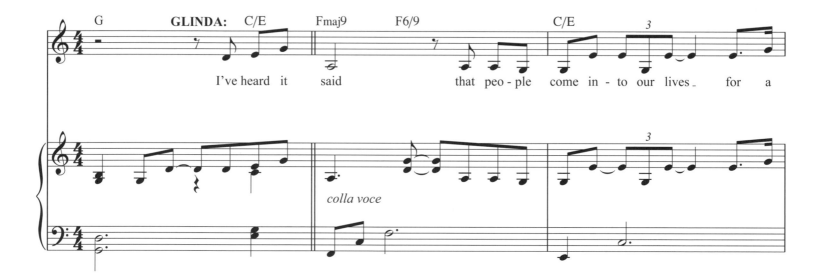

I've heard it said that peo-ple come in-to our lives for a

rea - son, bring-ing some-thing we must learn. And we are led to those who

help us most to grow, _ if we let them, _____ and we help them in __ re - turn.

Well, I don't know if I be - lieve that's true, ____ But I

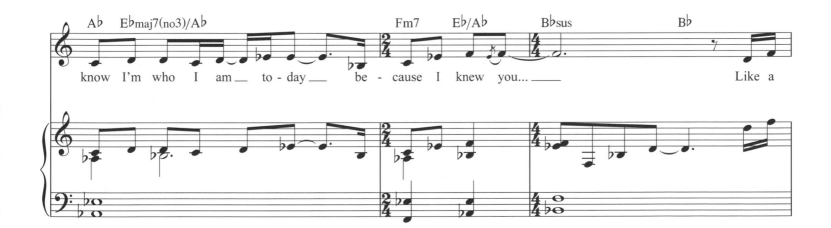

know I'm who I am __ to - day __ be - cause I knew you... _____ Like a

com - et pulled from or - bit as it pass - es a sun, ____ like a

stream that meets a boul - der half - way _____ through the wood, _____

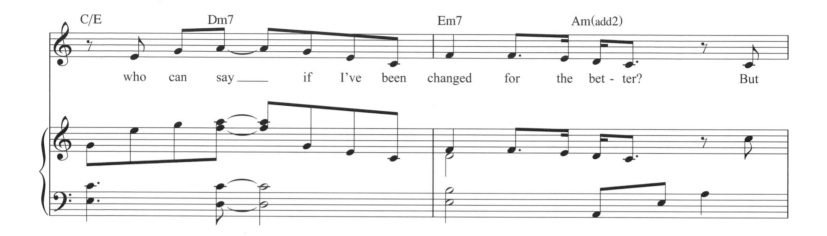

who can say _____ if I've been changed for the bet - ter? But

be - cause I knew you, I have been changed for

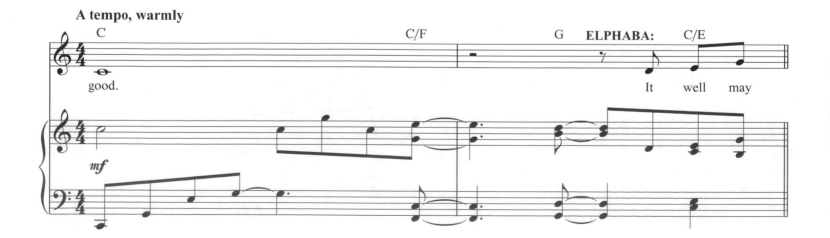

A tempo, warmly

good. **ELPHABA:** It well may

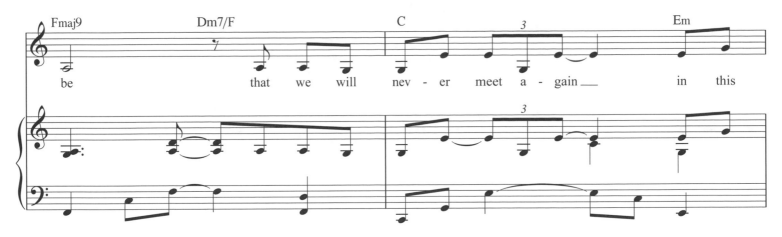

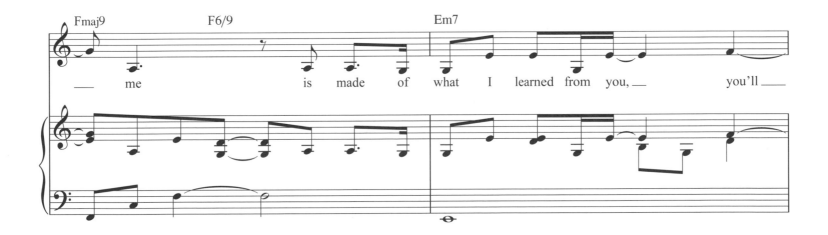

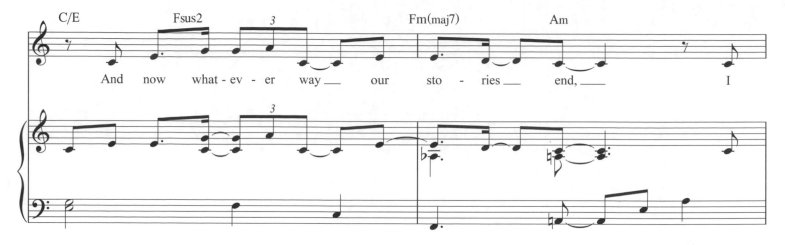

And now what-ev-er way ___ our sto-ries ___ end, ___ I

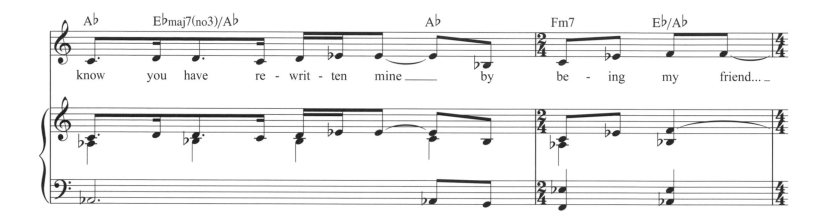

know you have re-writ-ten mine ___ by be-ing my friend... ___

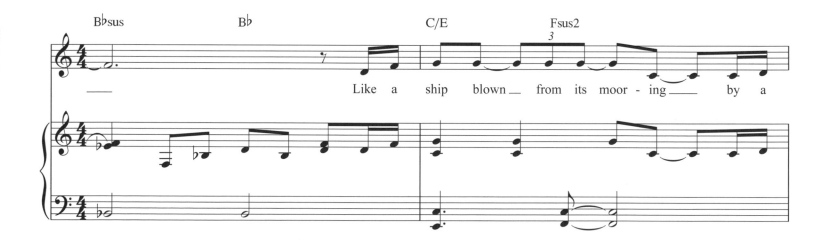

___ Like a ship blown ___ from its moor-ing ___ by a

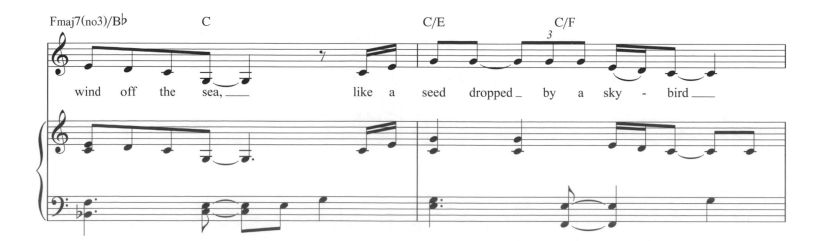

wind off the sea, ___ like a seed dropped ___ by a sky - bird ___

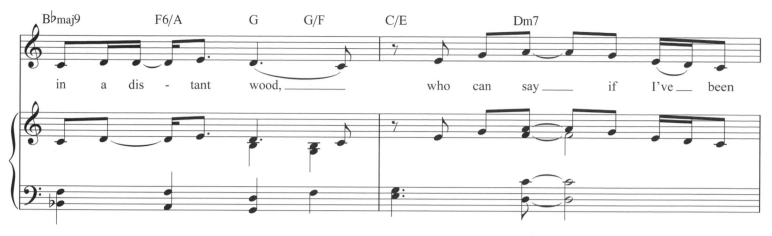

in a dis - tant wood, _____ who can say ____ if I've __ been

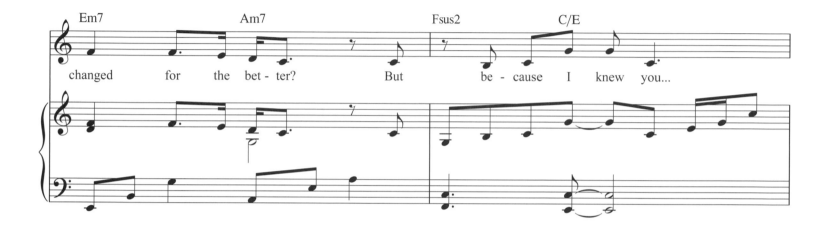

changed for the bet - ter? But be - cause I knew you...

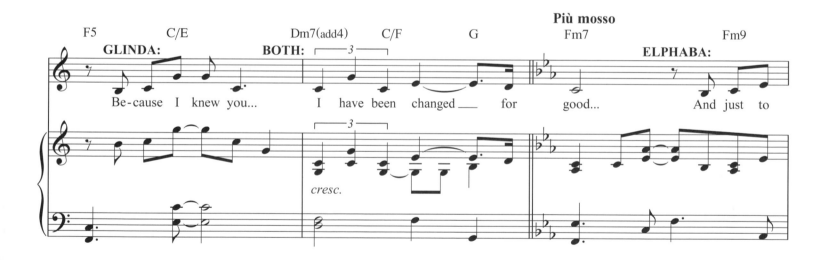

Più mosso

GLINDA: Be-cause I knew you... **BOTH:** I have been changed __ for good... **ELPHABA:** And just to

clear the air, I ask for - give - ness for the things I've done __ you

58

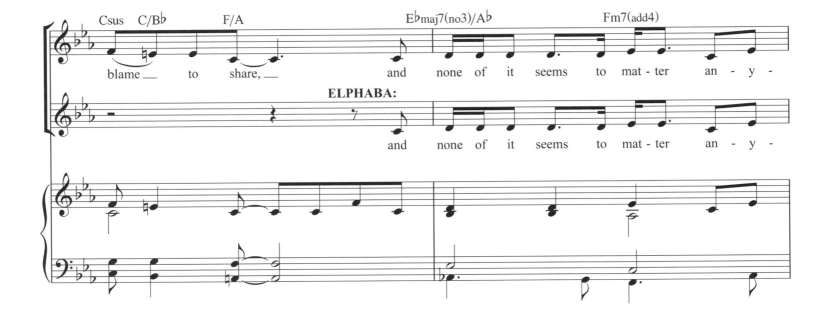

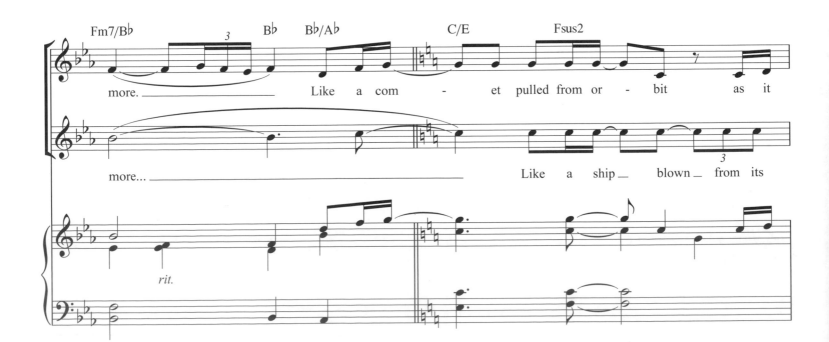

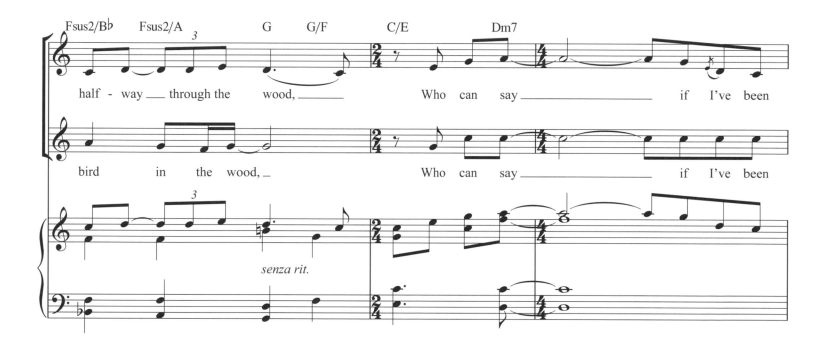

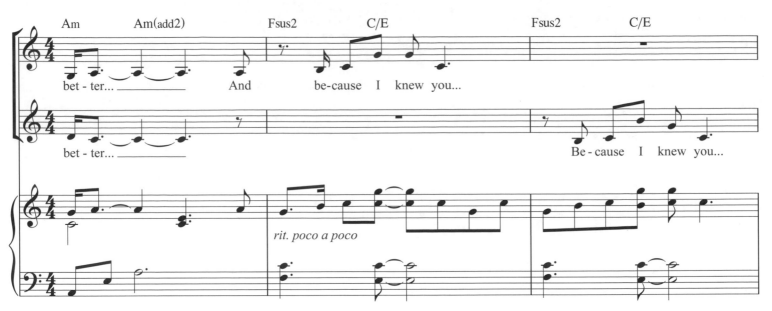

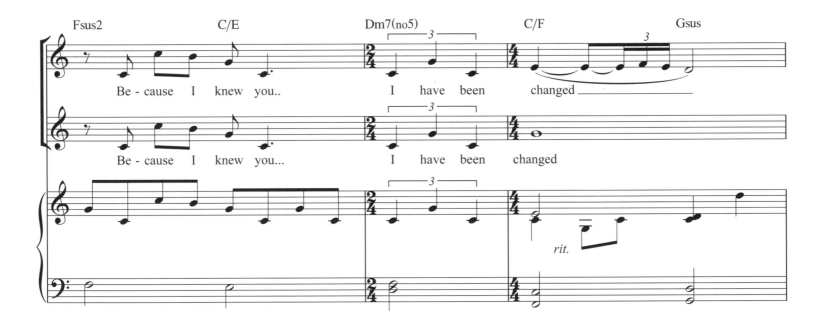

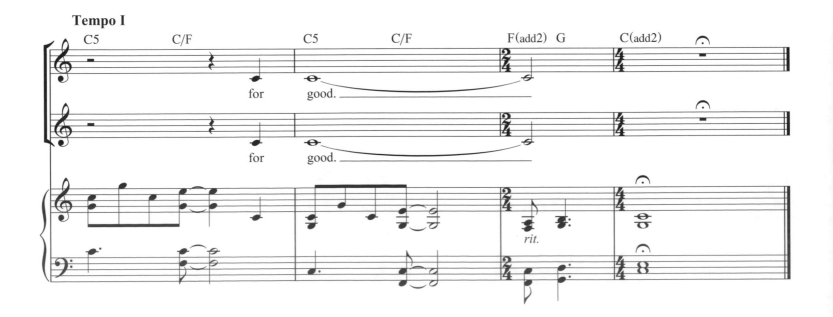

I GOT THE SUN IN THE MORNING

from the Stage Production ANNIE GET YOUR GUN

Words and Music by
IRVING BERLIN

Light bounce

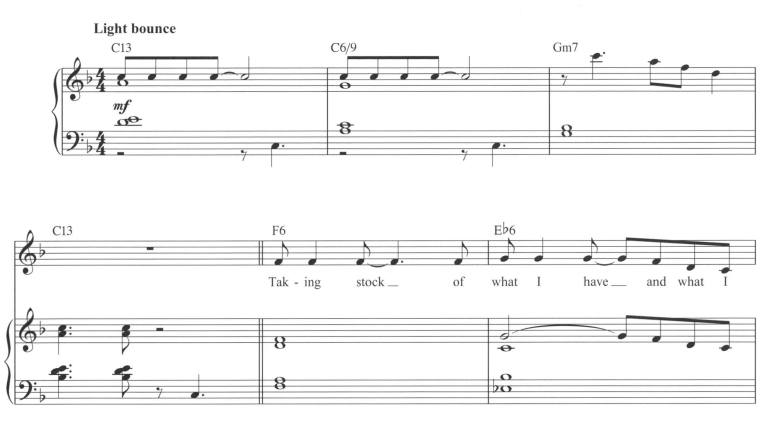

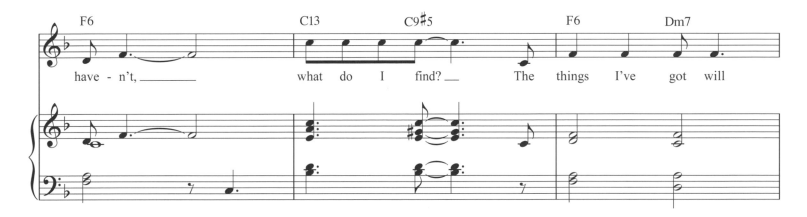

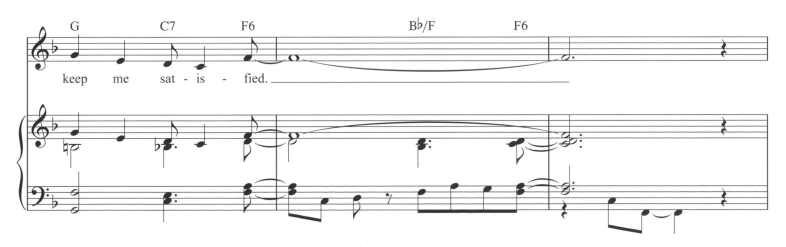

Moderate jump tempo

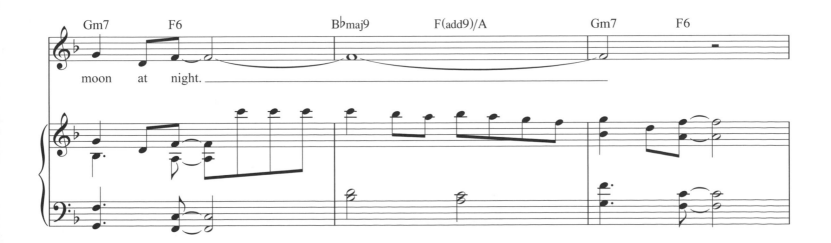

64

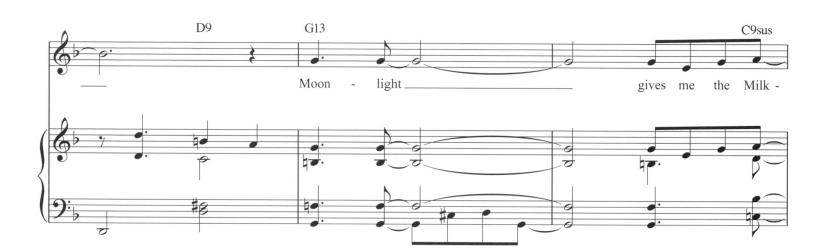

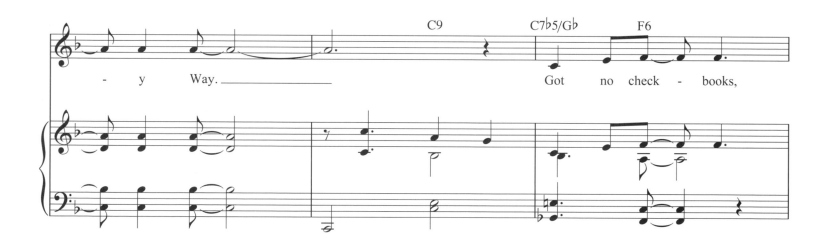

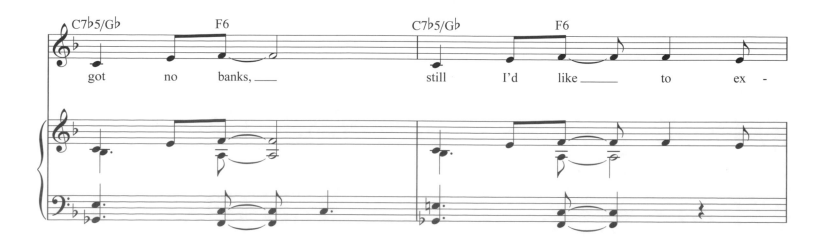

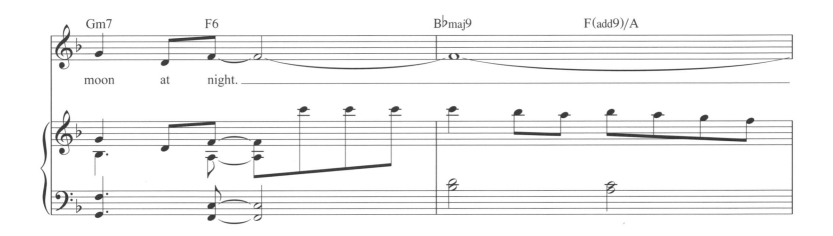

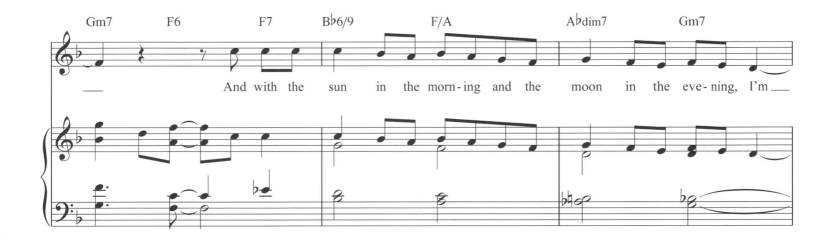

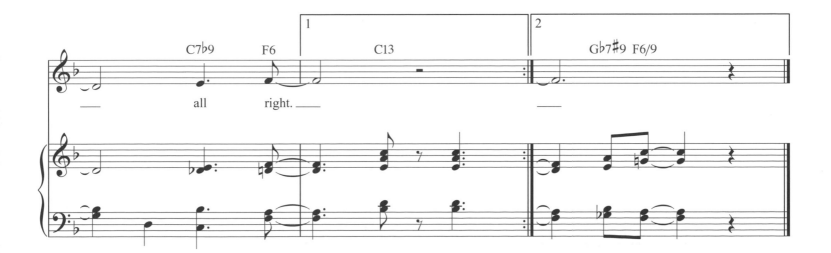

GETTING TO KNOW YOU

from THE KING AND I

Lyrics by OSCAR HAMMERSTEIN II
Music by RICHARD RODGERS

It's a ver-y an-cient say-ing But a true and hon-est thought, That if you be-come a teach-er, by your pu-pils you'll be taught. As a teach-er, I've been

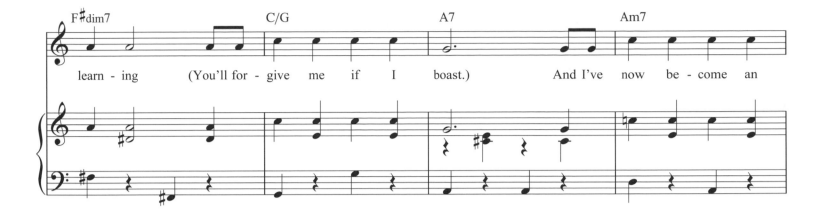

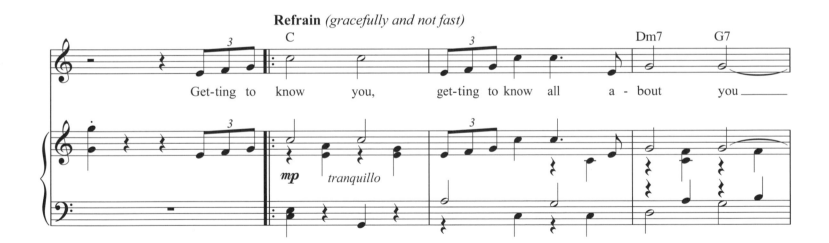

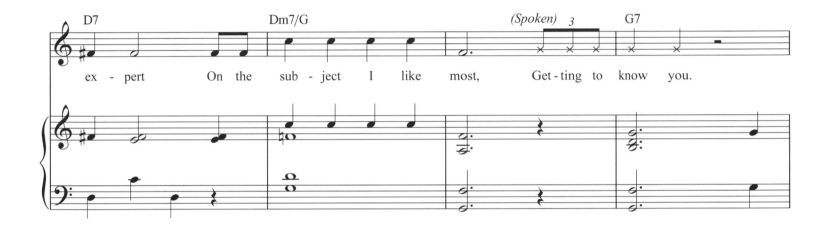

Get-ting to know you, Put-ting it my way, but nice - ly ____

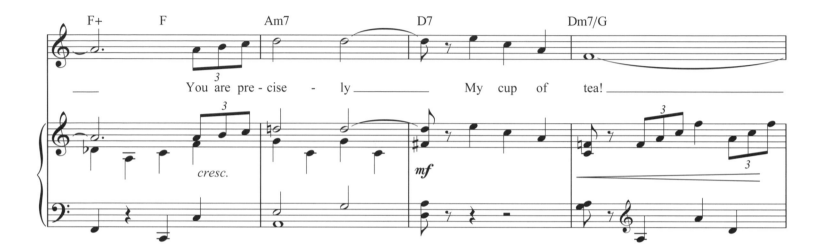

____ You are pre - cise - ly ____ My cup of tea! ____

____ Get-ting to know you, get-ting to feel free and eas - y ____

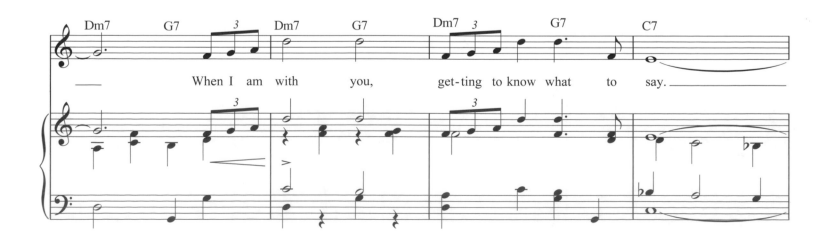

____ When I am with you, get-ting to know what to say. ____

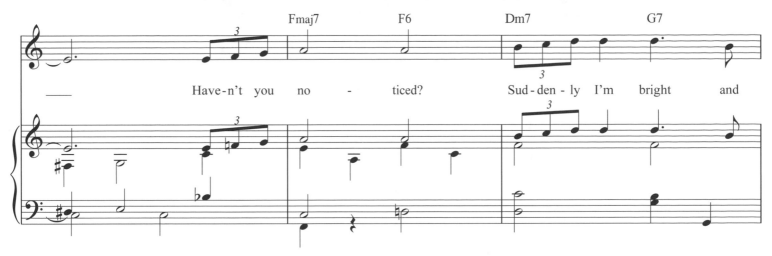

Have-n't you no - ticed? Sud-den-ly I'm bright and

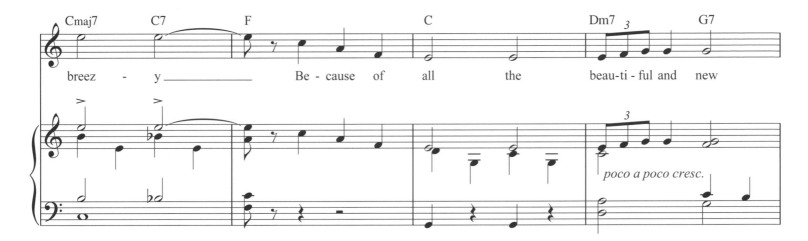

breez - y _____ Be - cause of all the beau-ti - ful and new

things I'm learn-ing a - bout you day by

day. _____ Get-ting to day. _____

GOODNIGHT, MY SOMEONE

from Meredith Willson's THE MUSIC MAN

By MEREDITH WILLSON

Good - night, my some - one, good - night, my love; sleep tight, my some - one, sleep tight, my love. Our star is shin - ing its bright - est light for good - night, my love, for good -

night. _____ Sweet dreams be yours, dear, if dreams there

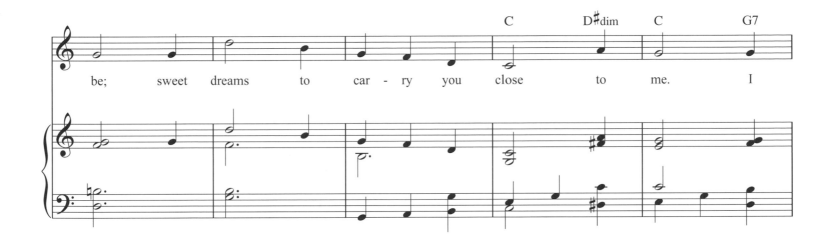

be; sweet dreams to car - ry you close to me. I

wish they may and I wish they might. Now good - night, my

some - one, good - night. Good - night. _____

I COULD HAVE DANCED ALL NIGHT

from MY FAIR LADY

Words by ALAN JAY LERNER
Music by FREDERICK LOEWE

Brightly

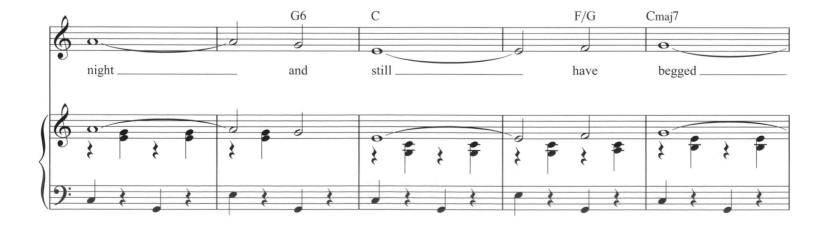

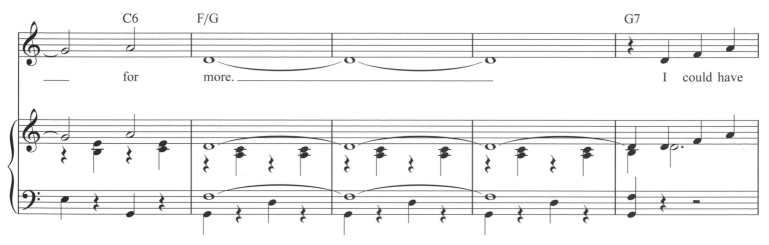

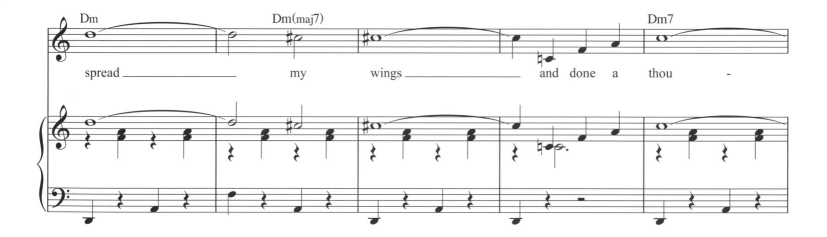

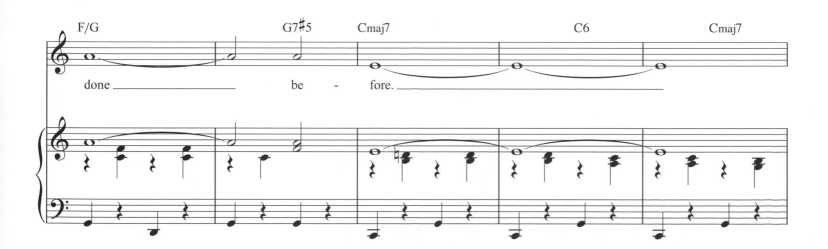

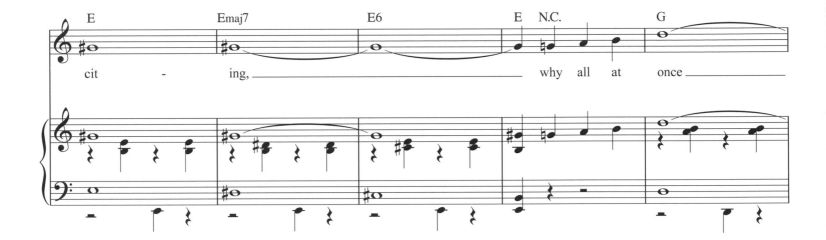

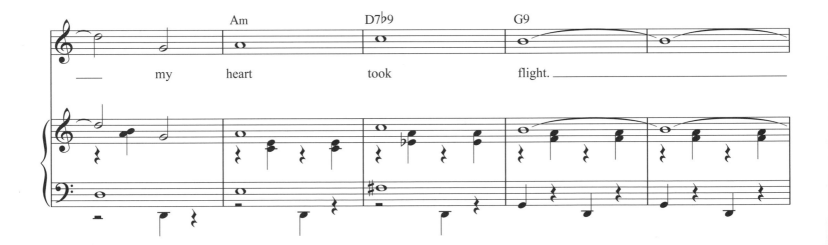

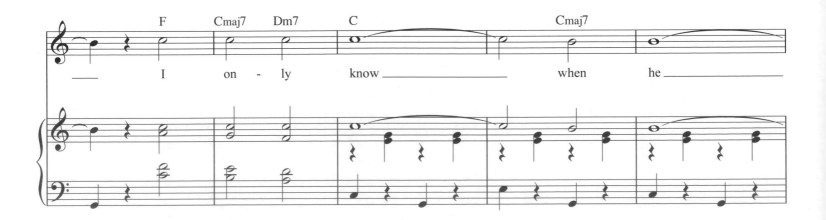

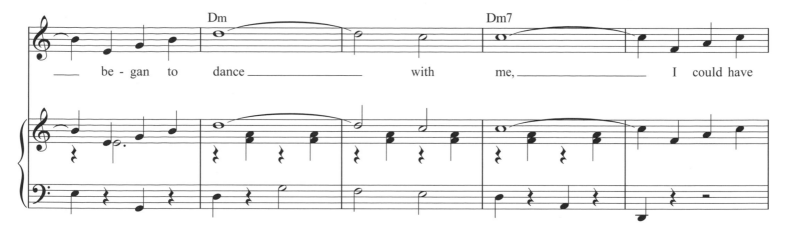

be - gan to dance _____ with me, _____ I could have

danced, danced, danced _____

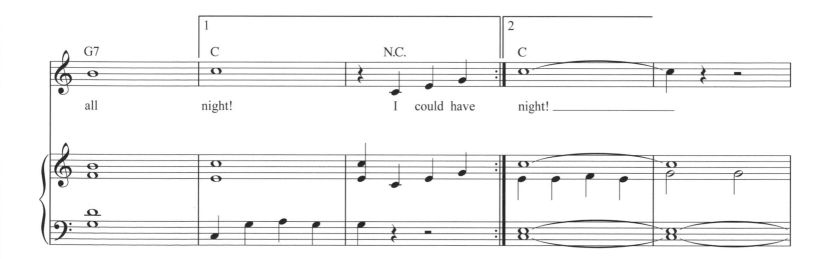

all night! I could have night! _____

I DON'T KNOW HOW TO LOVE HIM

from JESUS CHRIST SUPERSTAR

Words by TIM RICE
Music by ANDREW LLOYD WEBBER

Slowly, tenderly and very expressively

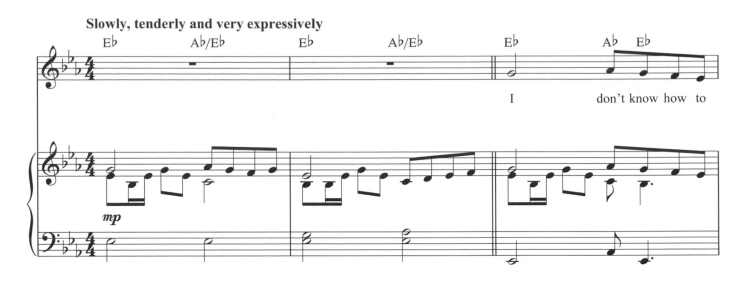

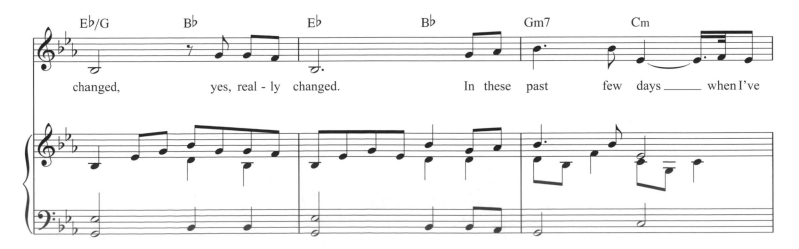

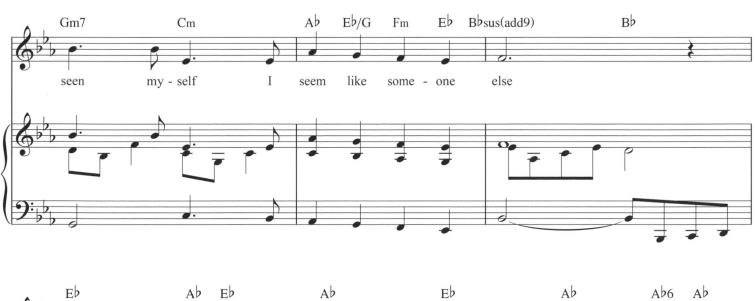

seen my - self I seem like some - one else

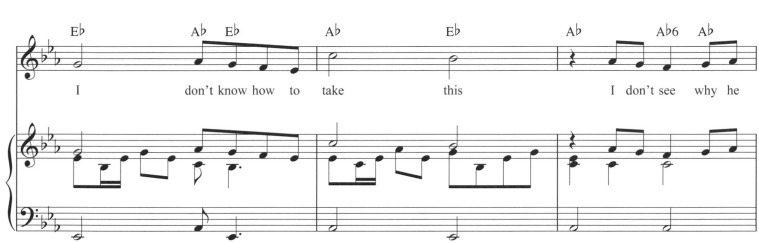

I don't know how to take this I don't see why he

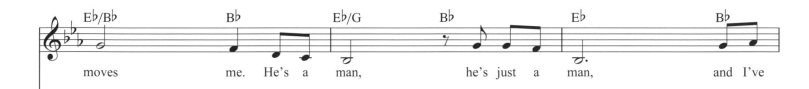

moves me. He's a man, he's just a man, and I've

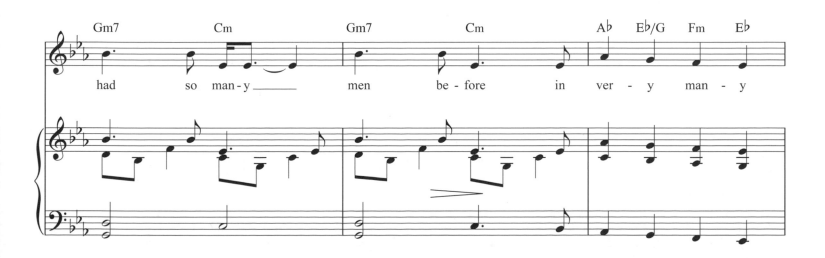

had so man - y men be - fore in ver - y man - y

ways.   He's just one   more.   Should I bring him   down __
Instrumental

__ should I scream and   shout? __   Should I speak of   love, __   let my feel - ings   out? __
Instrumental ends

__ I nev - er thought I'd   come to   this. __   What's it   all   a -

bout? _____   { Don't   you think it's rath - er
                                          { Yet   if   he said he

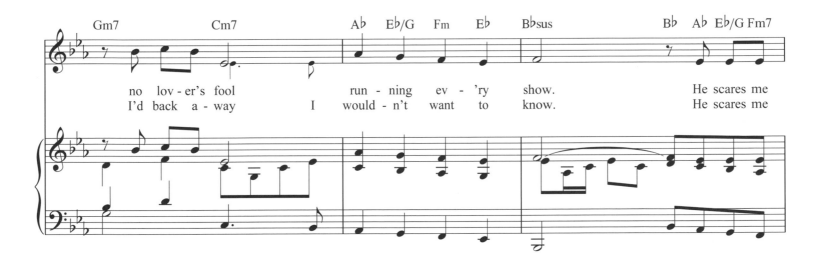

I DREAMED A DREAM

from LES MISÉRABLES

Music by CLAUDE-MICHEL SCHÖNBERG
Lyrics by ALAIN BOUBLIL, JEAN-MARC NATEL
and HERBERT KRETZMER

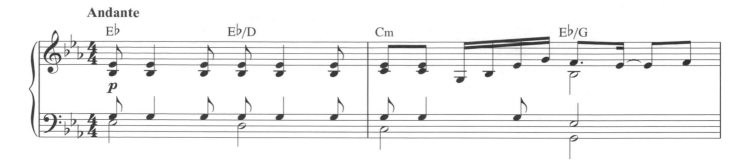

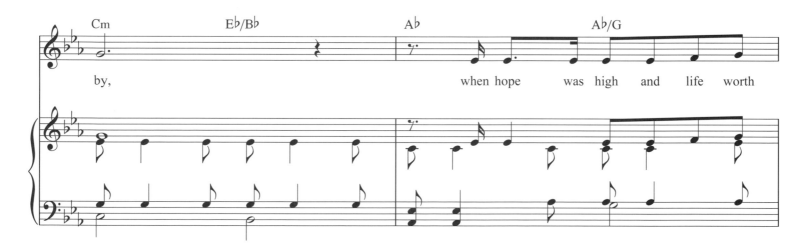

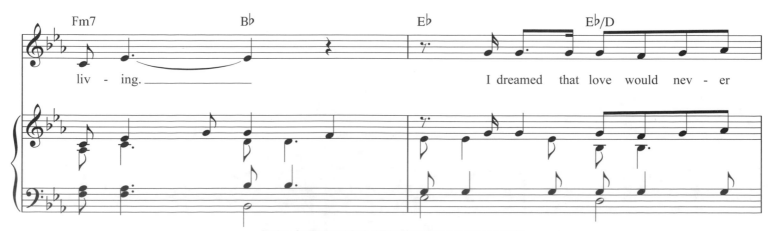

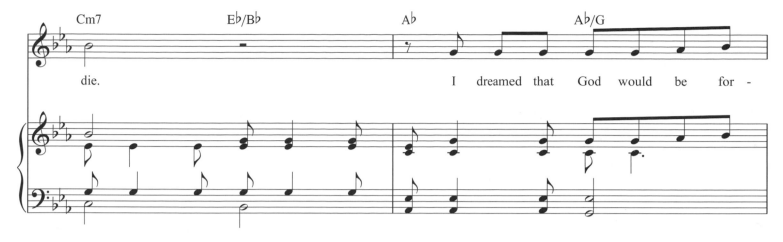

die.   I dreamed that God would be for -

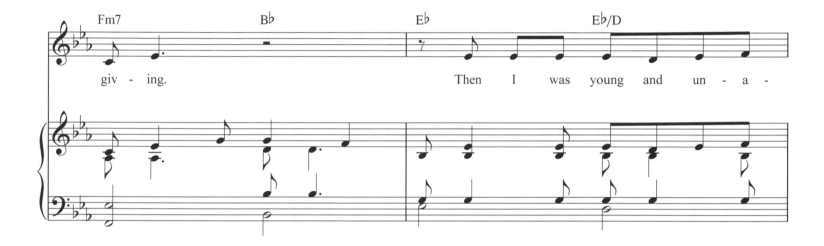

giv - ing.   Then I was young and un - a -

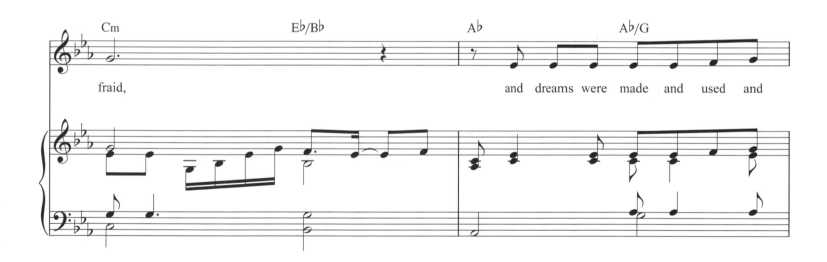

fraid,   and dreams were made and used and

wast - ed. _____   There was no ran - som to be

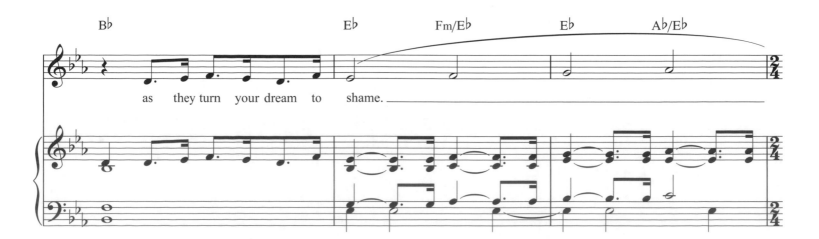

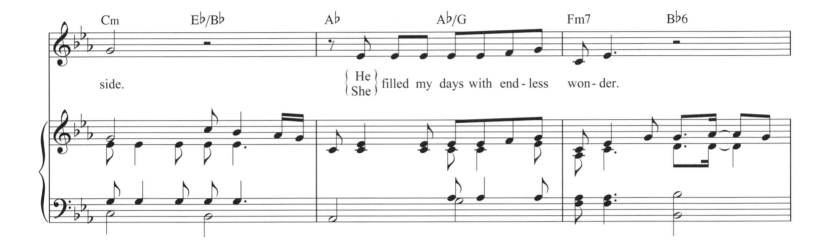

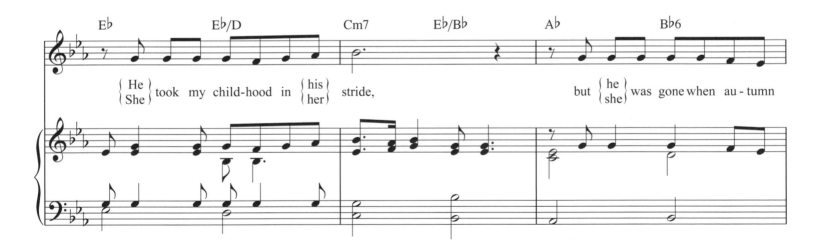

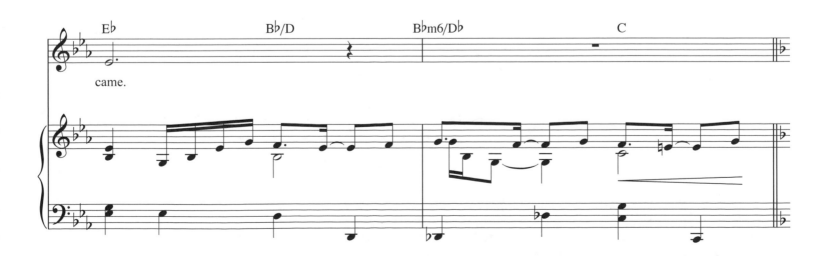

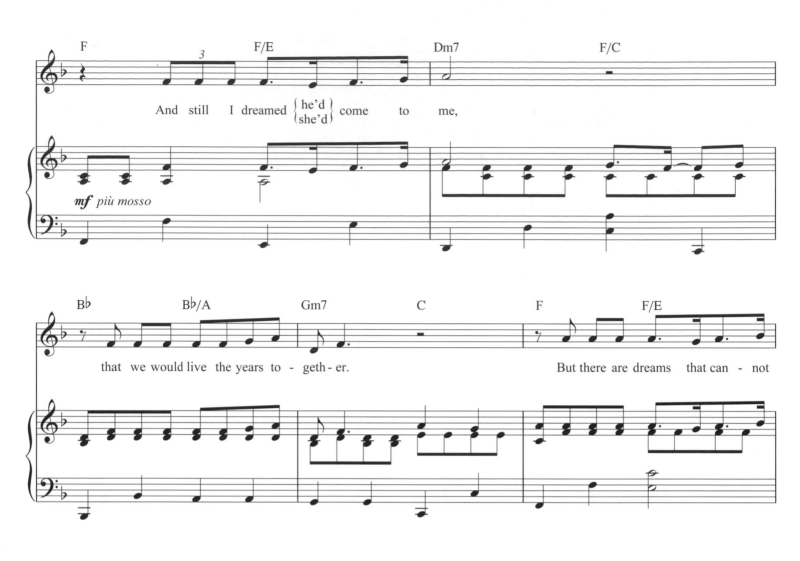

And still I dreamed {he'd}{she'd} come to me,

mf *più mosso*

that we would live the years to - geth - er.

But there are dreams that can - not

be,

and there are storms we can - not weath - er. _____

cresc.

I had a dream my life would

f *appassionato*

I FEEL PRETTY

from WEST SIDE STORY

Lyrics by STEPHEN SONDHEIM
Music by LEONARD BERNSTEIN

Brightly (alla Spagnola)

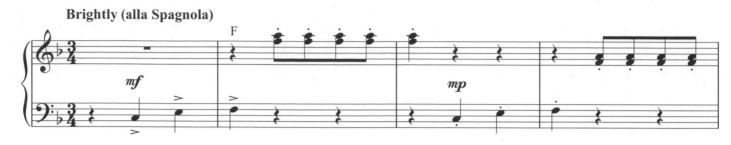

With pulse

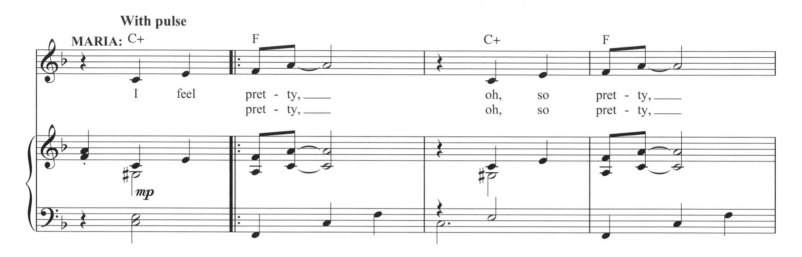

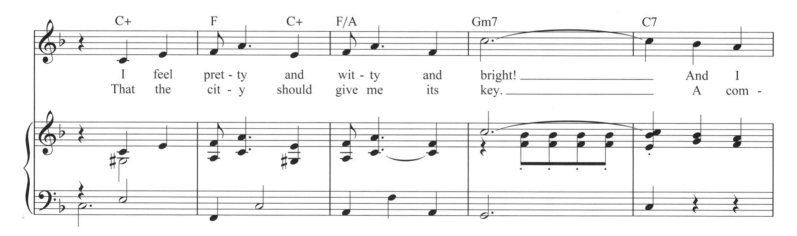

Originally an ensemble number, adapted here as a solo.

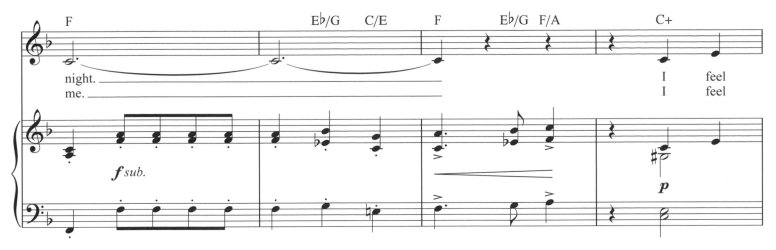

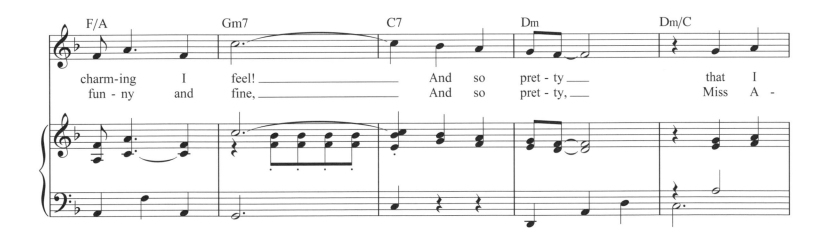

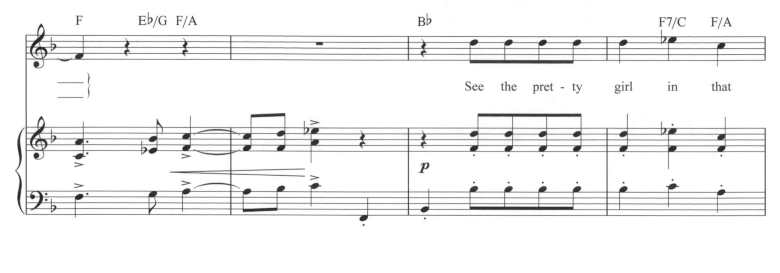

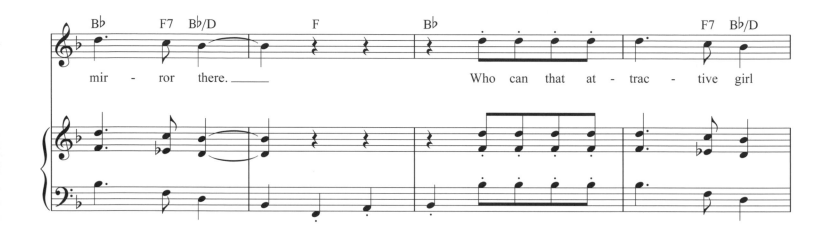

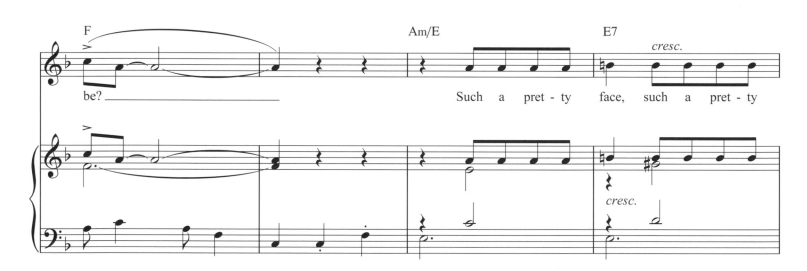

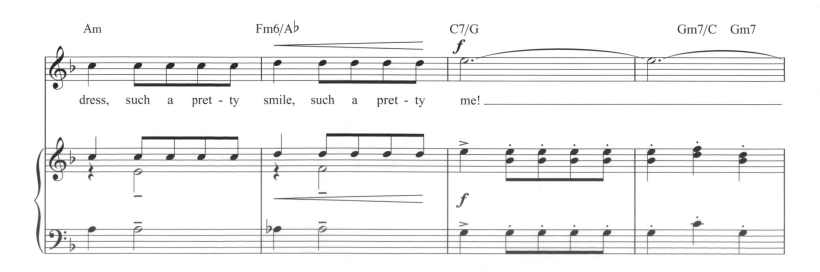

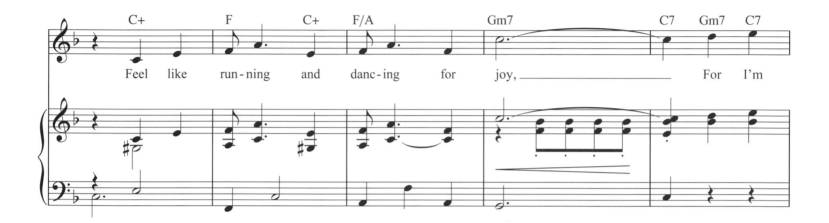

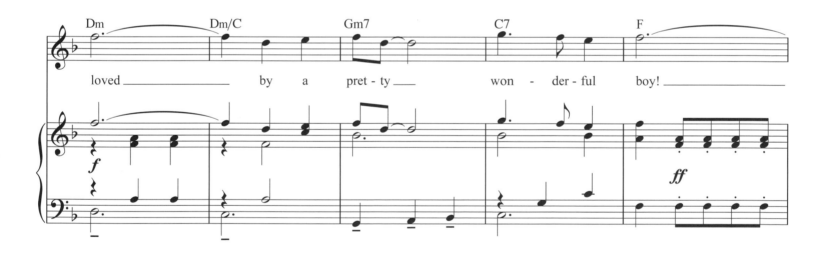

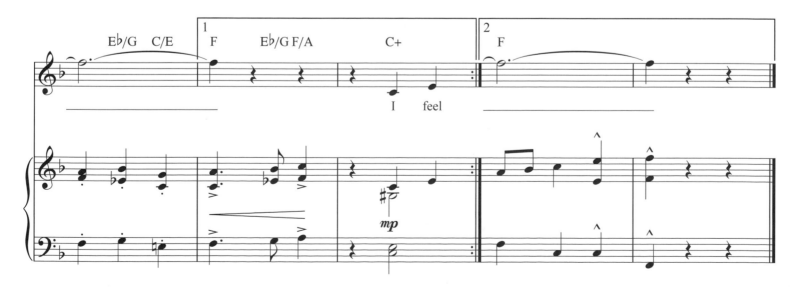

IF EVER I WOULD LEAVE YOU

from CAMELOT

Words by ALAN JAY LERNER
Music by FREDERICK LOEWE

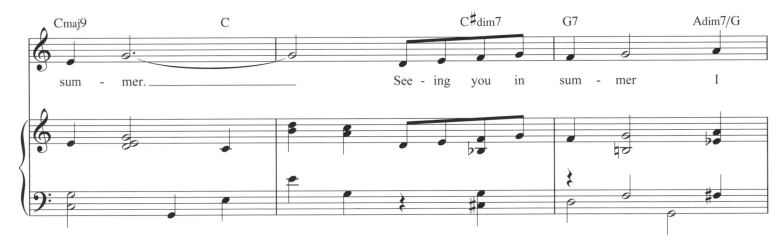

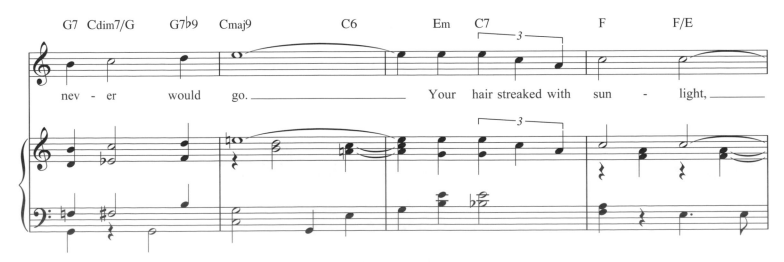

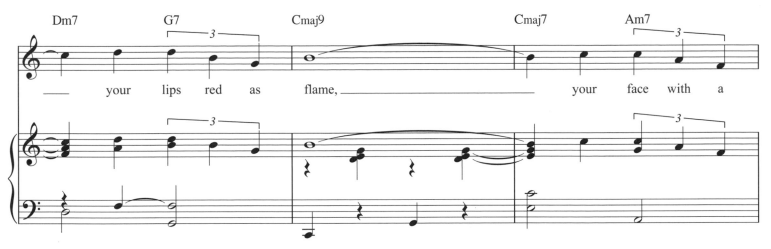

your lips red as flame, _____ your face with a

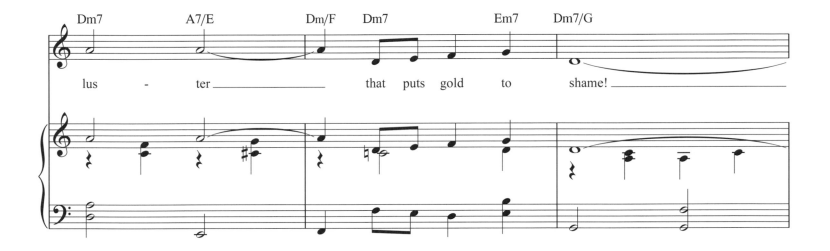

lus - ter _____ that puts gold to shame! _____

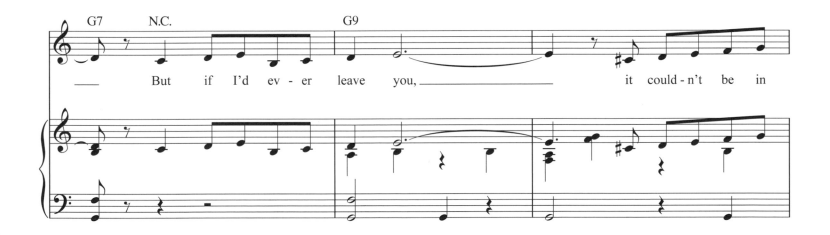

___ But if I'd ev - er leave you, _____ it could - n't be in

au - tumn. _____ How I'd leave in au - tumn I nev - er will

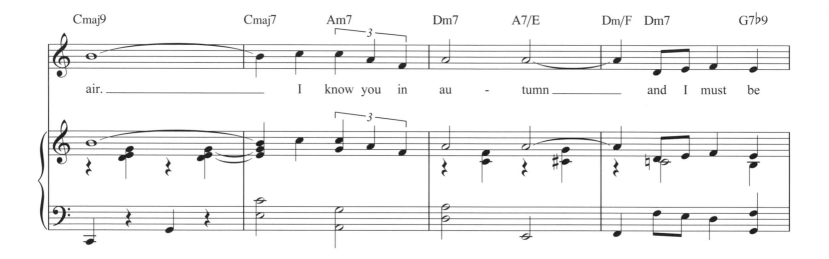

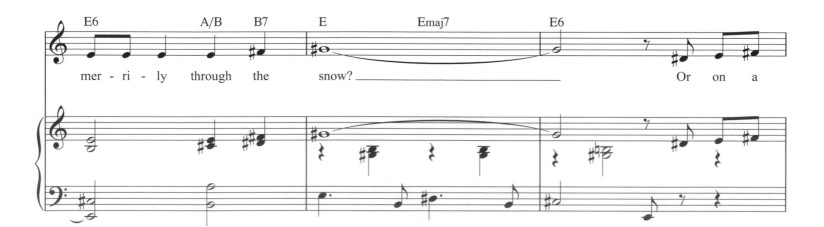

win - try eve - ning when you catch the fi - re's glow?

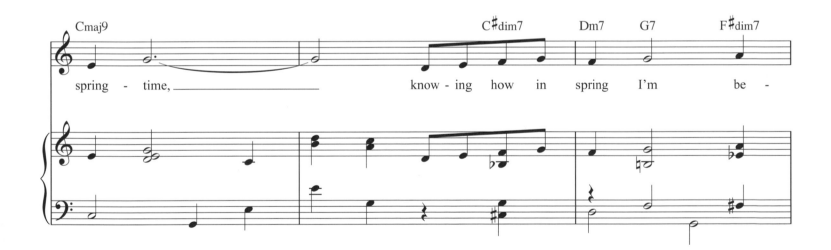

___ If ev - er I would leave you, ___ how could it be in

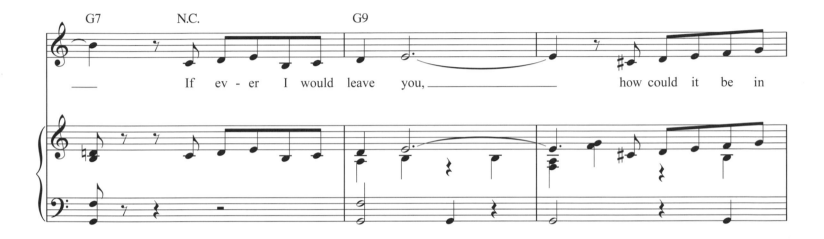

spring - time, ___ know - ing how in spring I'm be -

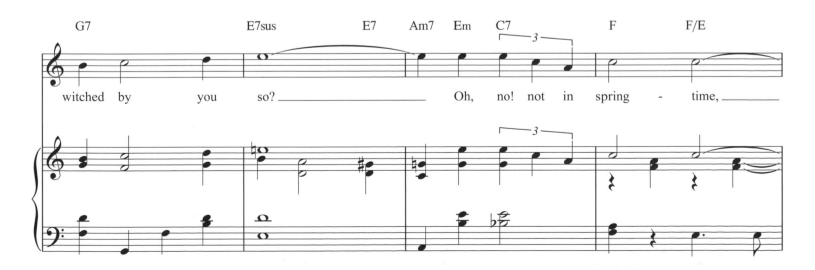

witched by you so? ___ Oh, no! not in spring - time, ___

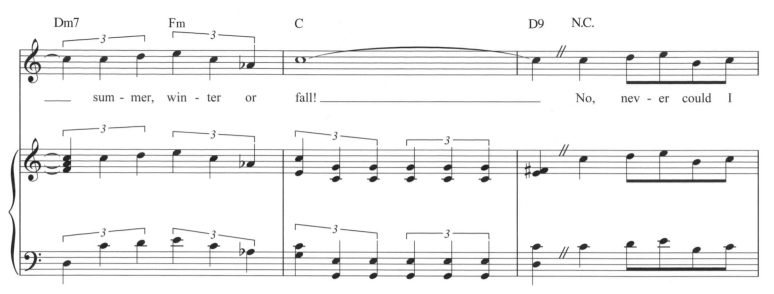

_____ sum - mer, win - ter or fall! _____ No, nev - er could I

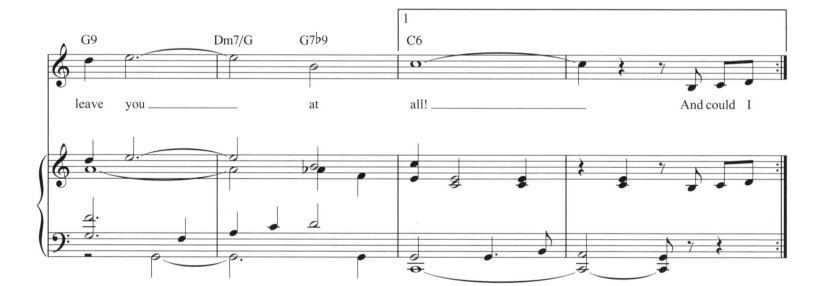

leave you _____ at all! _____ And could I

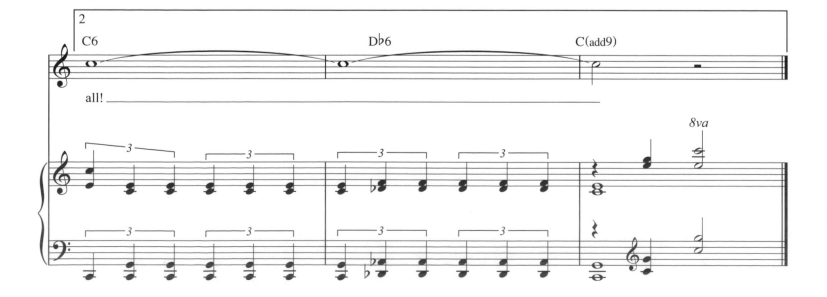

all! _____

MAKE BELIEVE

from SHOW BOAT

Lyrics by OSCAR HAMMERSTEIN II
Music by JEROME KERN

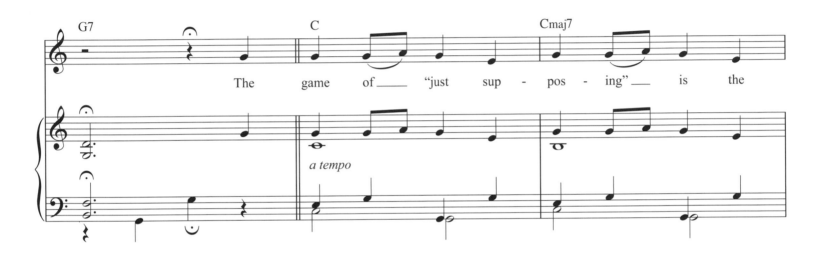

The game of "just sup - pos - ing" is the sweet - est game I know. Our dreams are

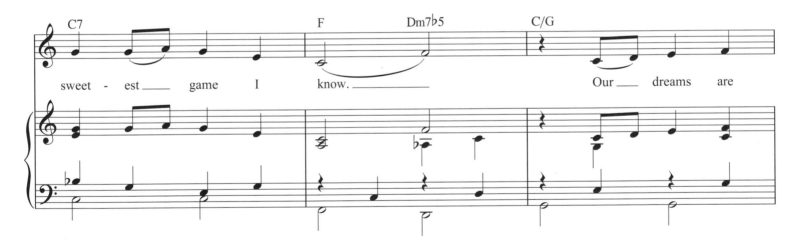

more ro - man - tic than the world we see.

And if the things we dream a - bout don't hap - pen __ to be

so, _____ that's __ just an un - im - por - tant

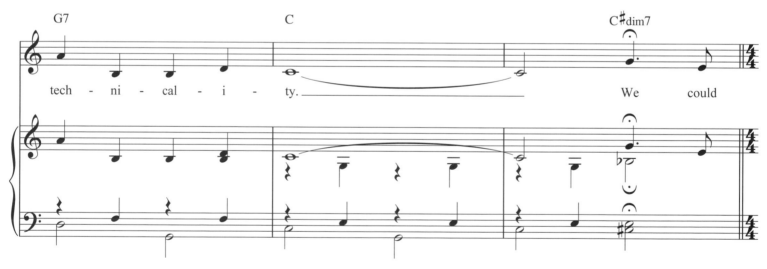

tech - ni - cal - i - ty. _____ We could

Slower

make be - lieve _____ I love you, _____ on - ly

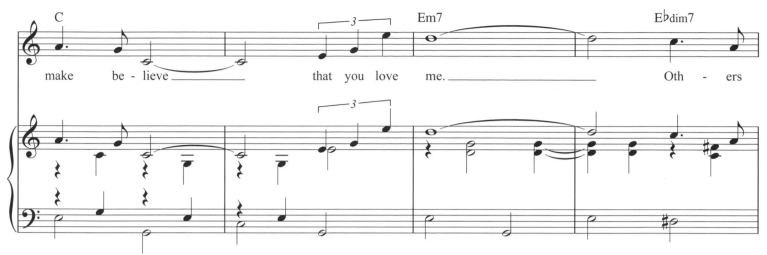

make be- lieve _____ that you love me. _____ Oth - ers

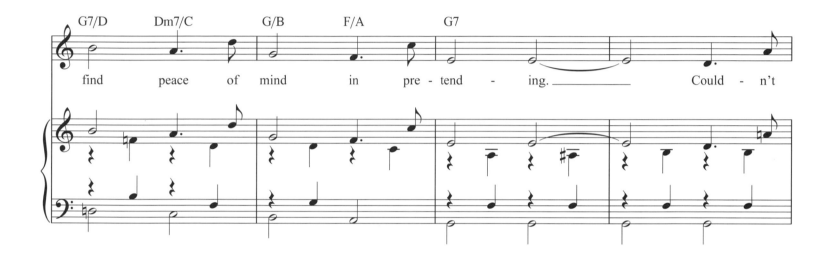

find peace of mind in pre - tend - ing. _____ Could - n't

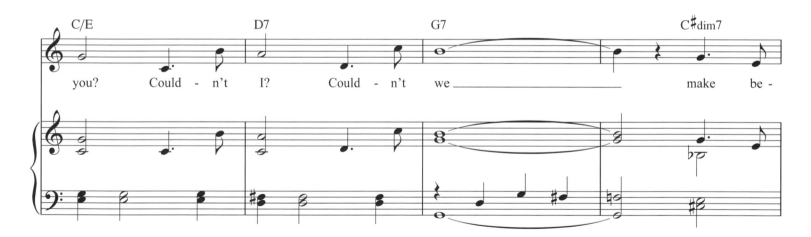

you? Could - n't I? Could - n't we _____ make be -

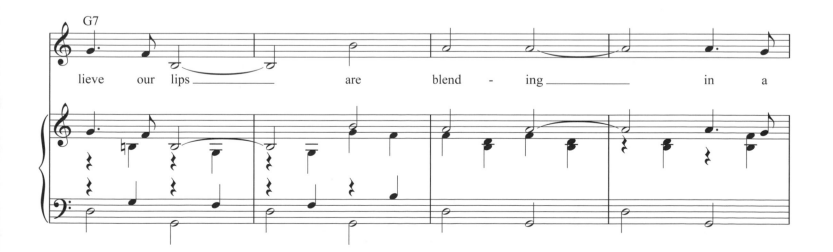

lieve our lips _____ are blend - ing _____ in a

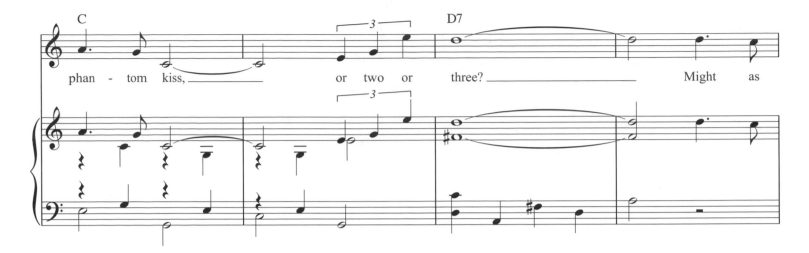

phan - tom kiss, _____ or two or three? _____ Might as

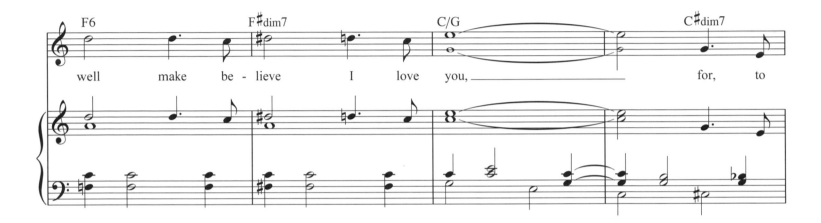

well make be - lieve I love you, _____ for, to

tell the truth, _____ I do. _____ We could

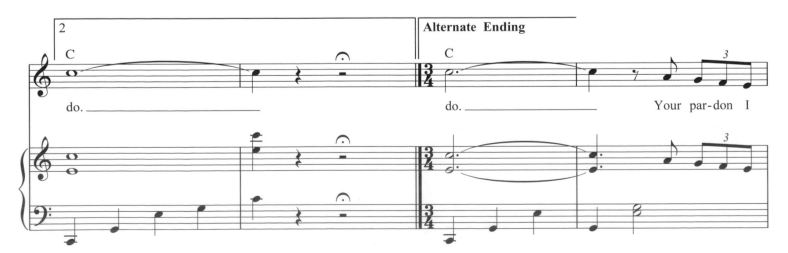

do. _____

Alternate Ending

do. _____ Your par-don I

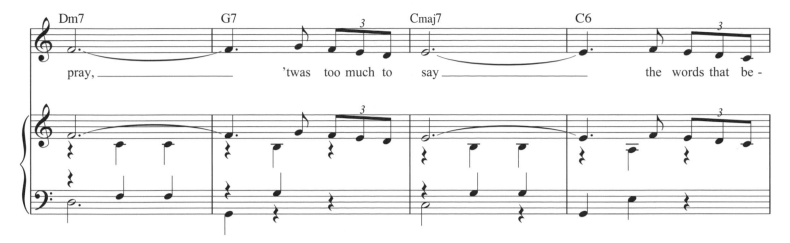

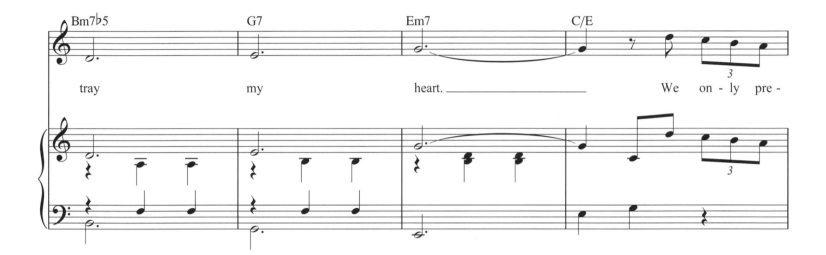

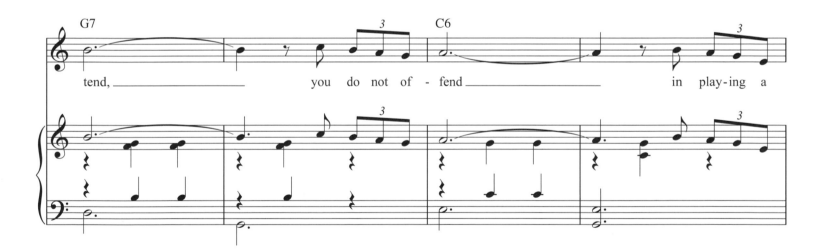

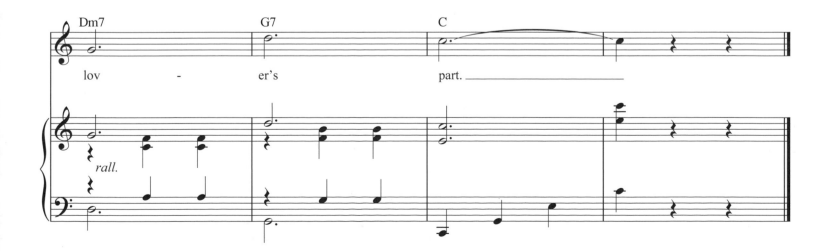

IF I LOVED YOU
from CAROUSEL

Lyrics by OSCAR HAMMERSTEIN II
Music by RICHARD RODGERS

If I loved you! Oh,
If I loved you! Oh,

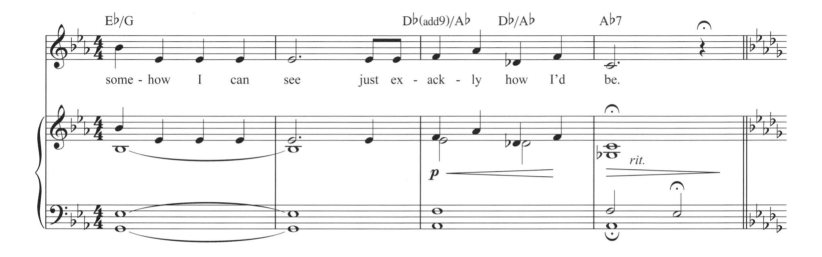

some - how I can see just ex - ack - ly how I'd be.

Refrain *(with great warmth, slowly)*

If I loved you, Time _ and a - gain _ I would try to say

All I'd want you to know. ___

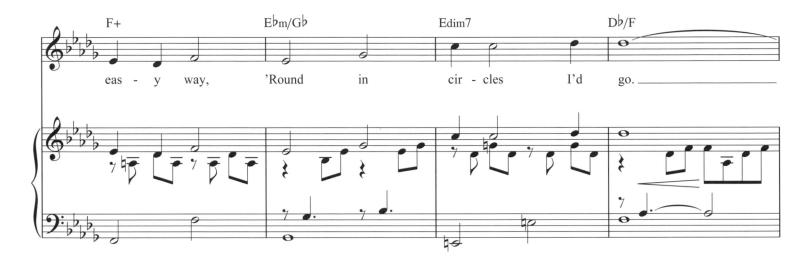

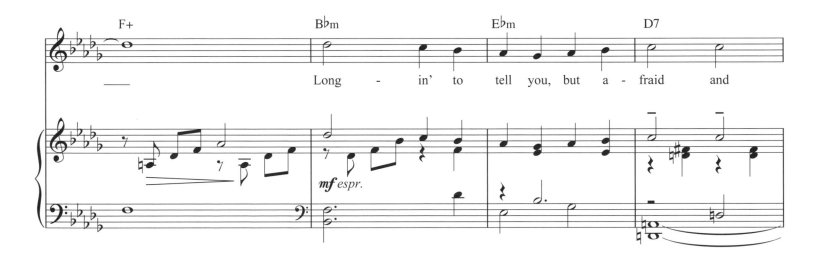

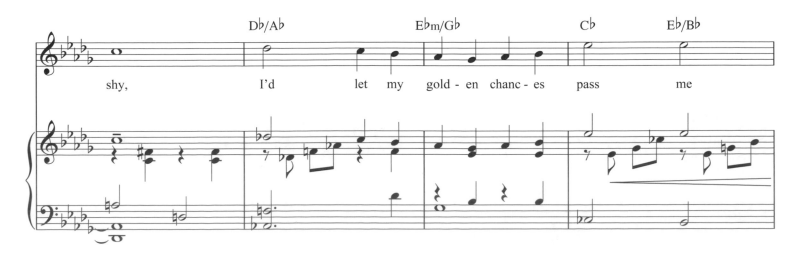

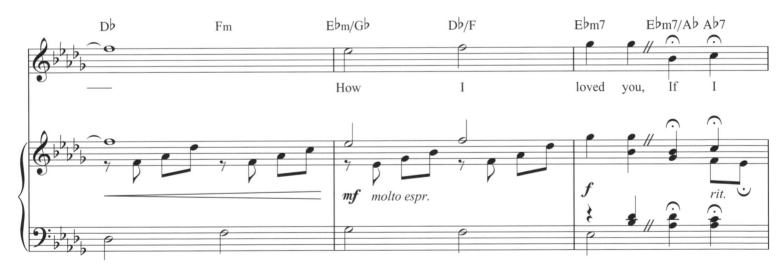

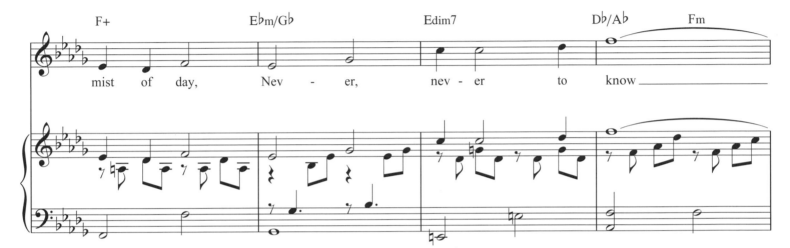

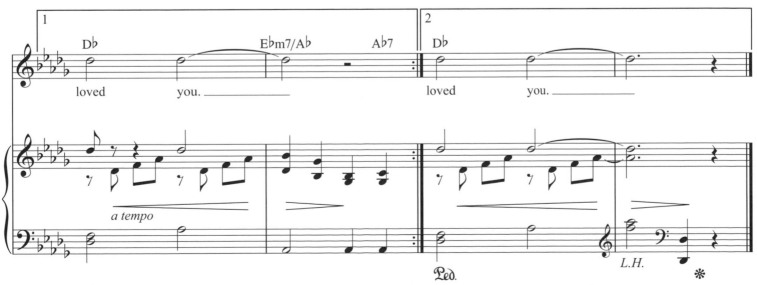

THE IMPOSSIBLE DREAM
(The Quest)
from MAN OF LA MANCHA

Lyric by JOE DARION
Music by MITCH LEIGH

Tempo di Bolero

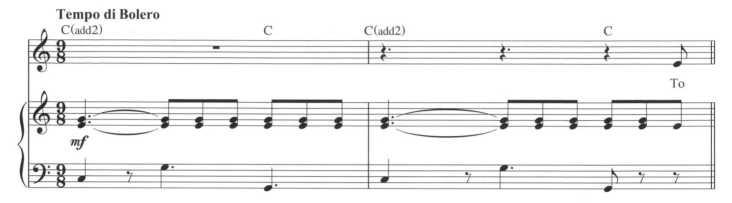

To

dream _____ the im-pos-si-ble dream, _____ to
right _____ the un-right-a-ble wrong, _____ to

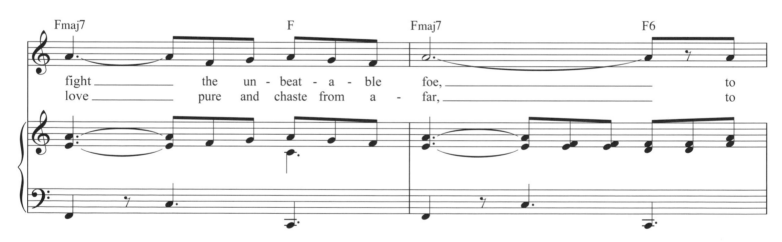

fight _____ the un-beat-a-ble foe, _____ to
love _____ pure and chaste from a - far, _____ to

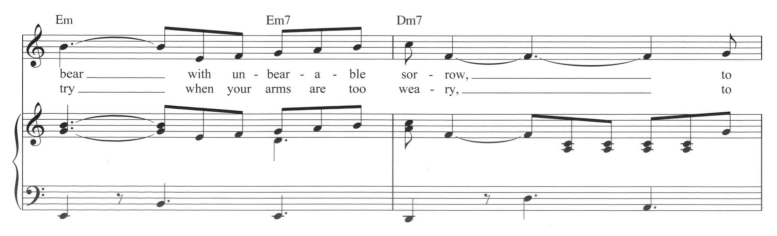

bear _____ with un-bear-a-ble sor - row, _____ to
try _____ when your arms are too wea-ry, _____ to

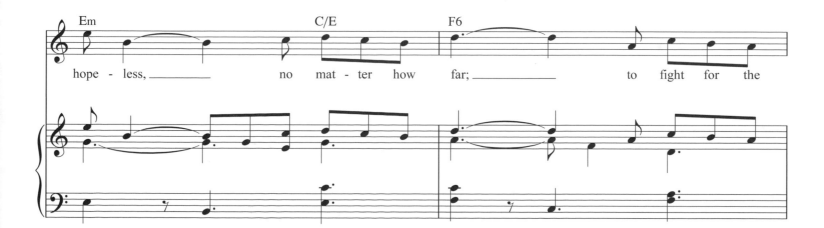

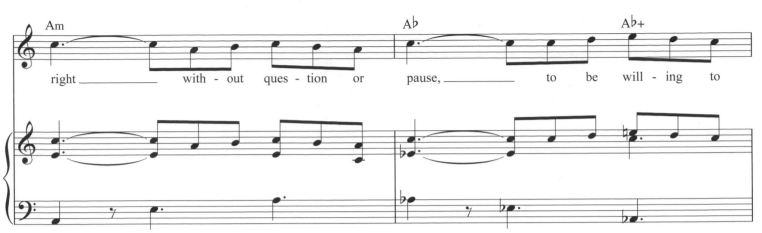

right _____ with - out ques - tion or pause, _____ to be will - ing to

march in - to hell for a heav - en - ly cause! And I know, _____ if I'll on - ly be

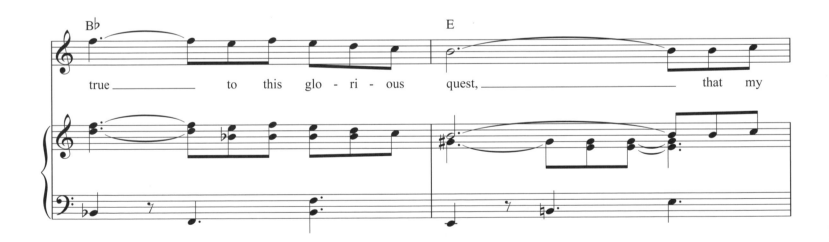

true _____ to this glo - ri - ous quest, _____ that my

heart _____ will lie peace - ful and calm _____ when I'm laid to my

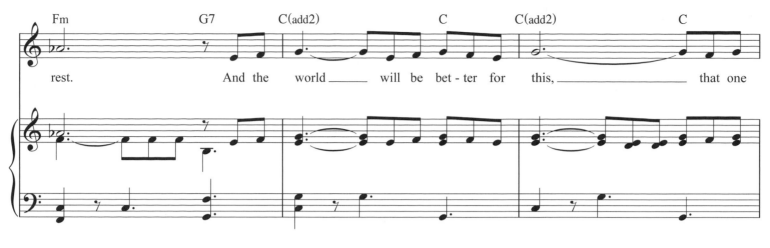

rest. And the world ____ will be bet-ter for this, ____ that one

man, ____ scorned and cov-ered with scars, ____ still ____

strove ____ with his last ounce of cour-age, ____ to

reach ____ the un-reach-a-ble stars. ____

LUCK BE A LADY

from GUYS AND DOLLS

By FRANK LOESSER

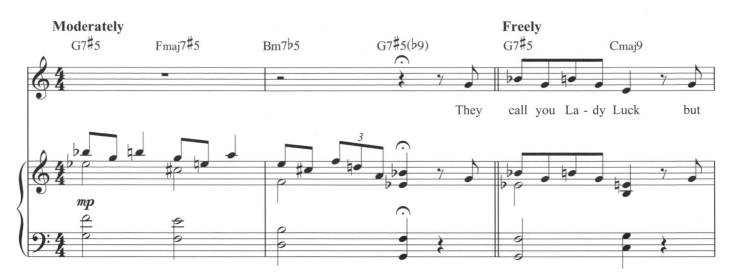

They call you La-dy Luck but

there is room for doubt. At times you have a ver-y un-la-dy like way of run-ning out. __ You're

on a date with me, the pick-ings have been lush, and yet be-fore this eve-ning is o-ver, you

might give me the brush. _ You might for-get your man-ners, you might re-fuse to stay, and

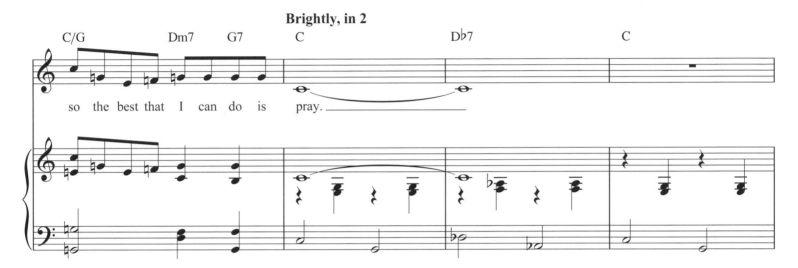

Brightly, in 2

so the best that I can do is pray. _

Luck be a la-dy to - night. _

_ Luck be a la-dy to - night. _

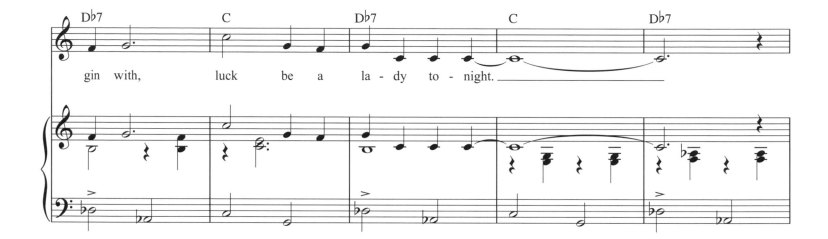

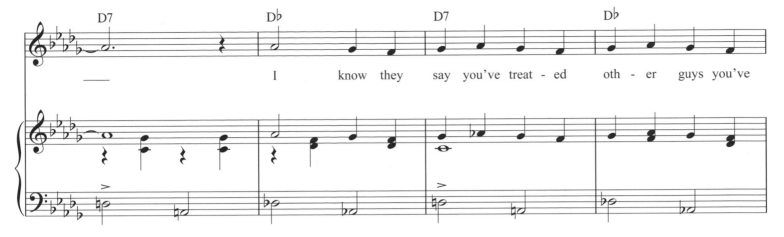

I know they say you've treat - ed oth - er guys you've

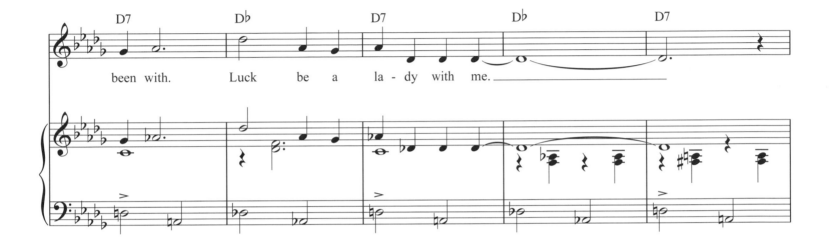

been with. Luck be a la - dy with me._____

A la - dy does - n't leave her

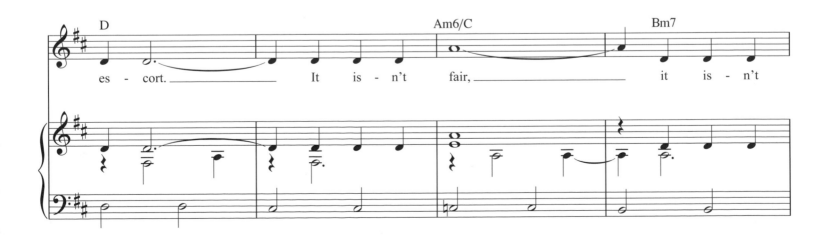

es - cort. _____ It is - n't fair, _____ it is - n't

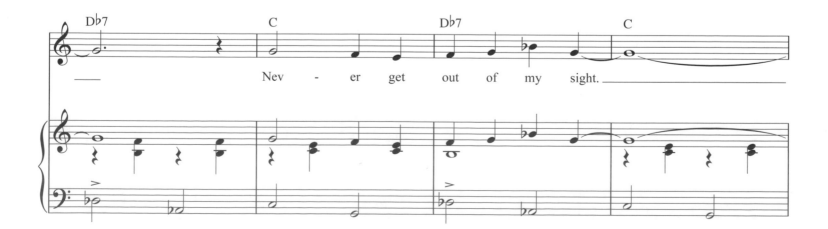

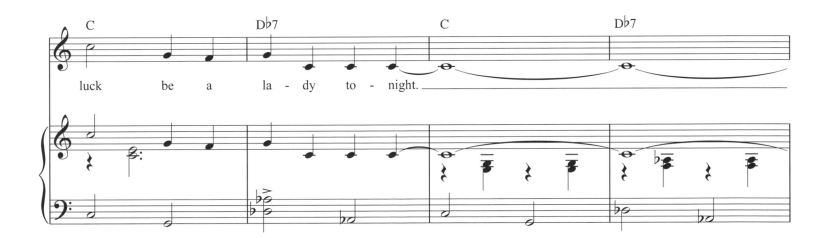

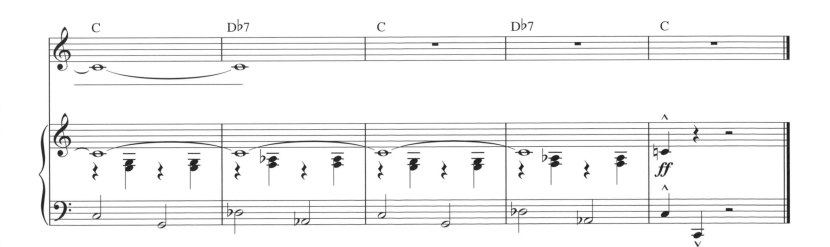

THE MAN I LOVE

from LADY BE GOOD
from STRIKE UP THE BAND

Music and Lyrics by GEORGE GERSHWIN
and IRA GERSHWIN

When the mel - low moon be - gins to beam, Ev - 'ry night I

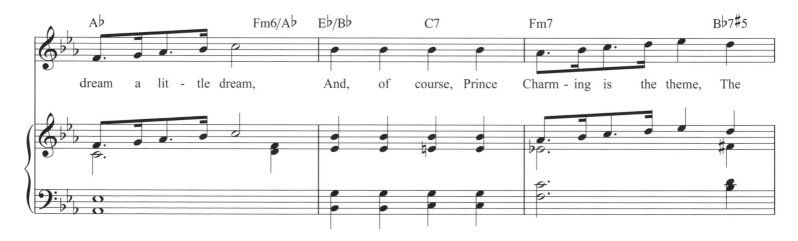

dream a lit - tle dream, And, of course, Prince Charm - ing is the theme, The

he for me. Al - though I re - al - ize as well as you,

It is sel-dom that a dream comes true, To me it's

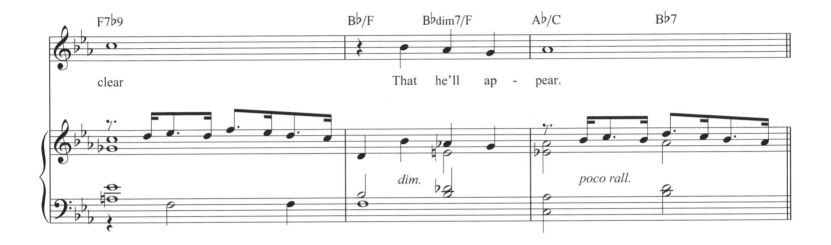

clear That he'll ap-pear.

Slow

Some-day he'll come a-long, The man I love; And he'll be big and strong,

p molto semplice e dolce

The man I love; And when he comes my way, I'll do my best to

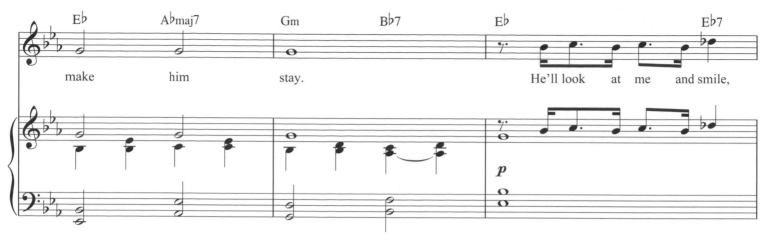

make him stay. He'll look at me and smile,

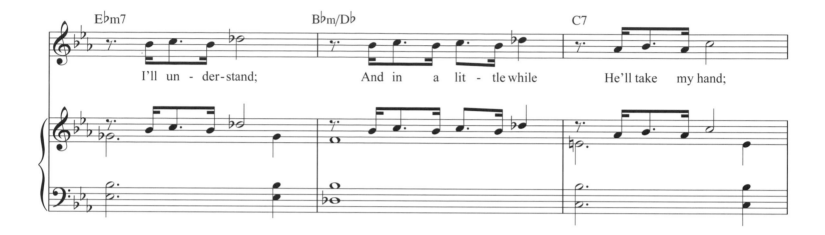

I'll un-der-stand; And in a lit-tle while He'll take my hand;

And though it seems ab-surd, I know we both won't say a

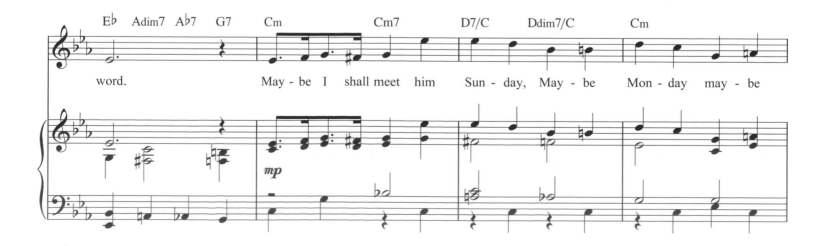

word. May-be I shall meet him Sun-day, May-be Mon-day may-be

not; Still I'm sure to meet him one day, May - be Tues - day will be

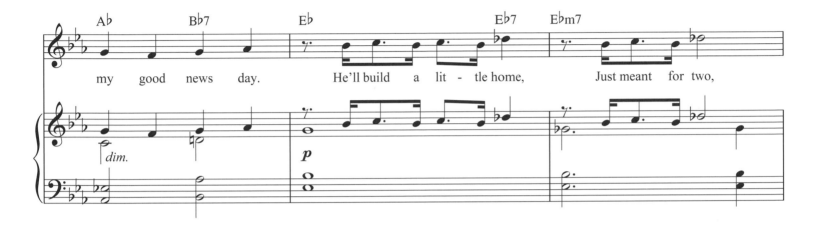

my good news day. He'll build a lit - tle home, Just meant for two,

From which I'll nev - er roam. Who would, would you? And so all else a - bove,

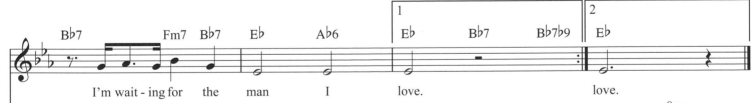

I'm wait - ing for the man I love. love.

MATCHMAKER

from the Musical FIDDLER ON THE ROOF

Words by SHELDON HARNICK
Music by JERRY BOCK

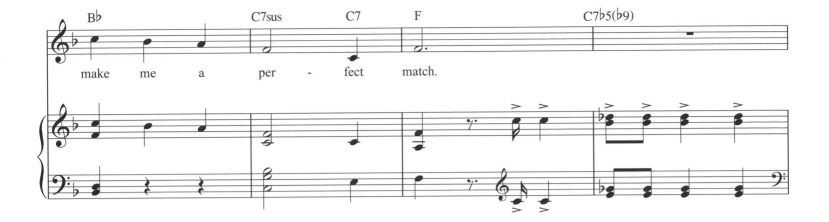

make me a per - fect match.

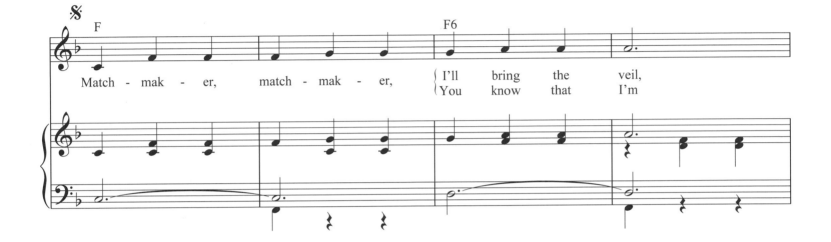

Match - mak - er, match - mak - er, { I'll bring the veil,
{ You know that veil I'm

You bring the groom, slen - der and pale;
still ver - y young, Please take your time;

Bring me a ring, for I'm long - ing to be the
Up to this min - ute, I mis - un - der - stood that

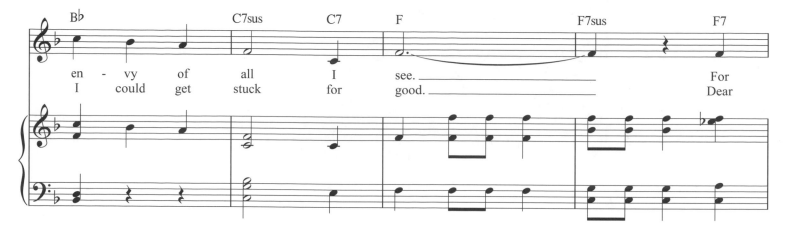

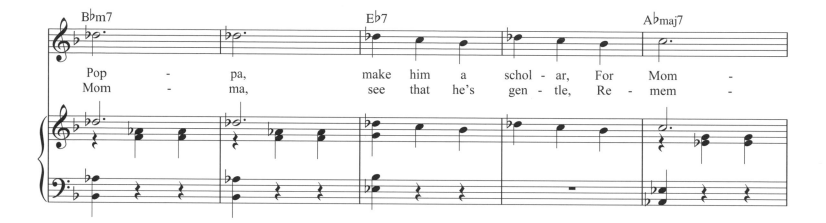

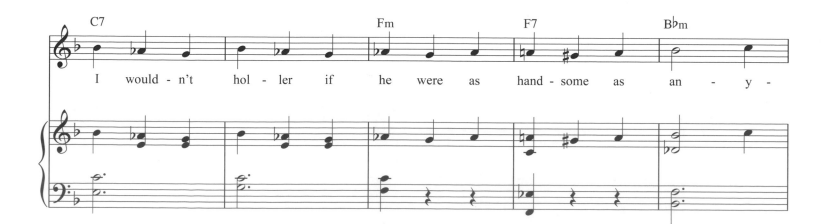

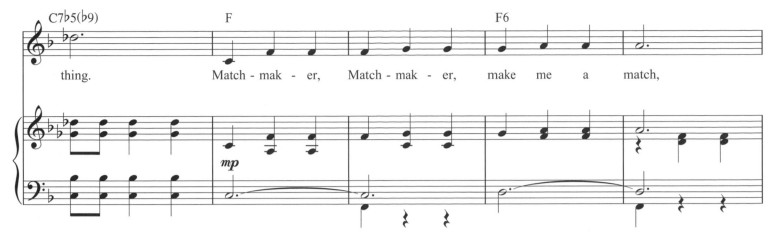

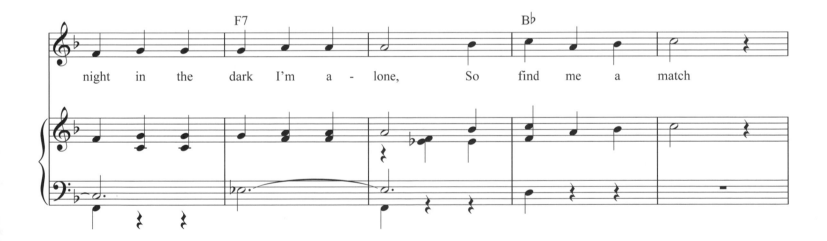

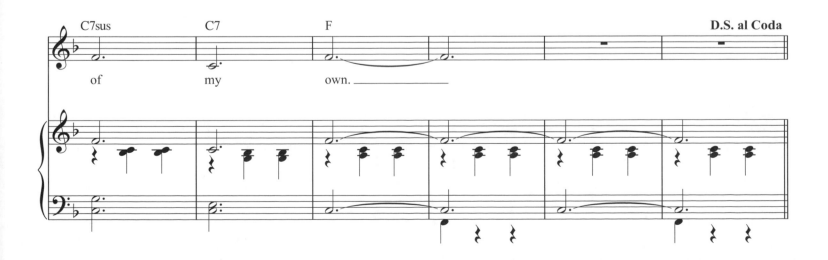

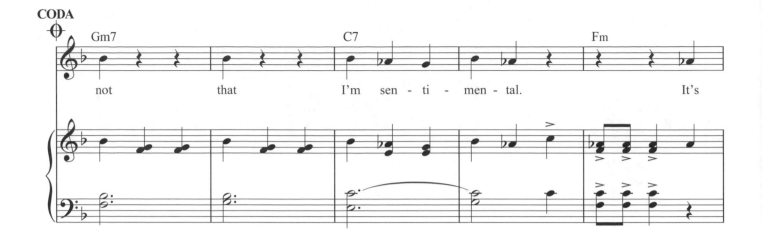

CODA

Gm7 / C7 / Fm

not that I'm sen - ti - men - tal. It's

F7 / Bbm / C7b5(b9)

just that I'm ter - ri - fied. _____

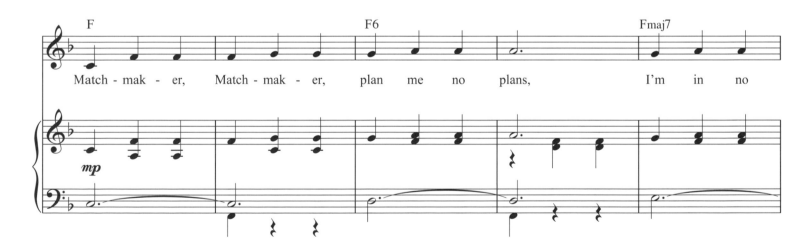

F / F6 / Fmaj7

Match - mak - er, Match - mak - er, plan me no plans, I'm in no

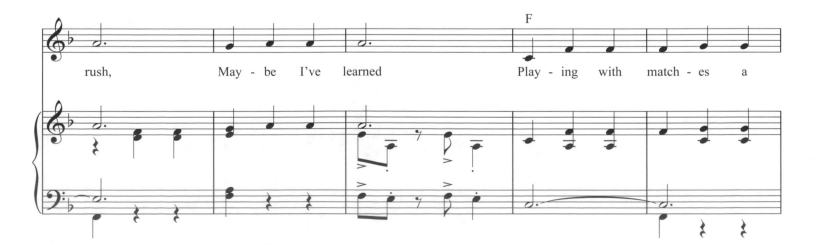

F

rush, May - be I've learned Play - ing with match - es a

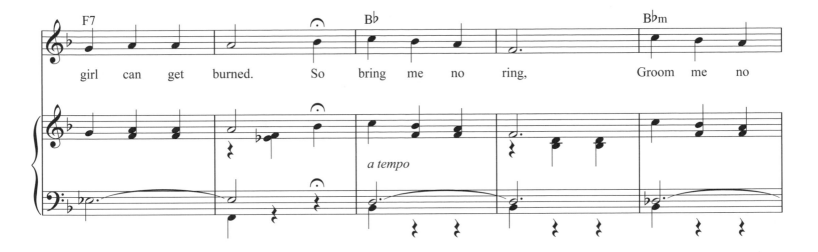

girl can get burned. So bring me no ring, Groom me no

groom, Find me no find, Catch me no catch;

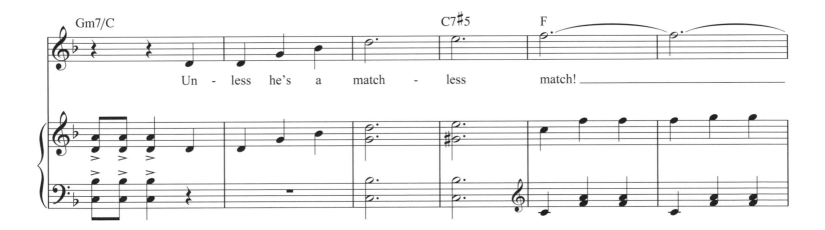

Un - less he's a match - less match! _____

MEMORY
from CATS

Music by ANDREW LLOYD WEBBER
Text by TREVOR NUNN after T.S. ELIOT

Mid - night._____ Not a sound from the pave - ment._____ Has the moon lost her
Mem - ory_____ all a - lone in the moon - light_____ I can smile at the

mem - ory?_____ She is smil-ing a - lone._____ In the
old days,_____ I was beau-ti-ful then._____ I re -

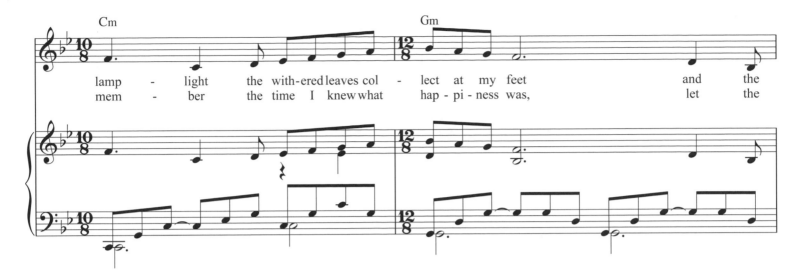

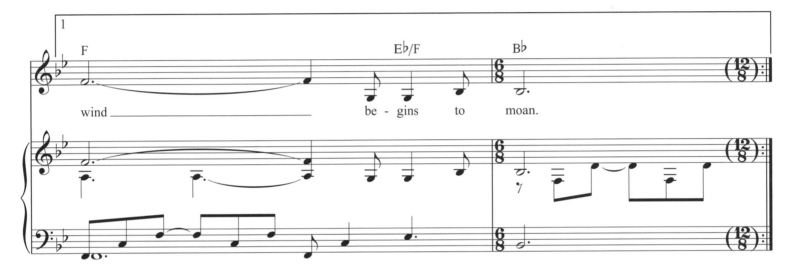

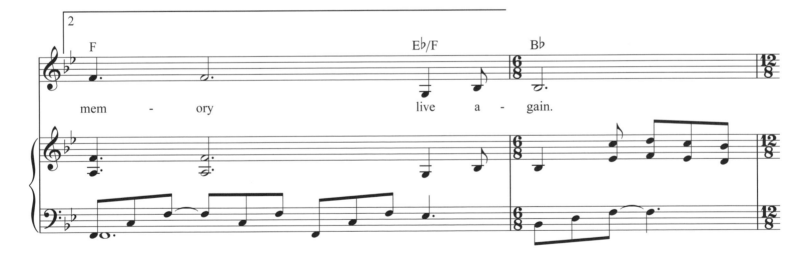

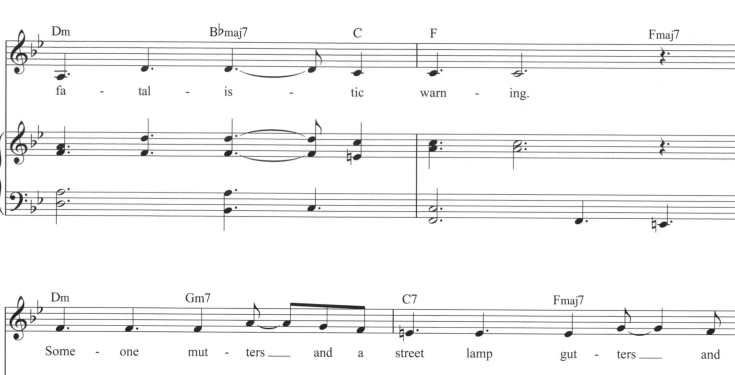

fa - tal - is - tic warn - ing.

Some - one mut - ters ___ and a street lamp gut - ters ___ and

soon it will be morn - ing.

rit.

Day - light. ___ I must wait for the sun - rise, ___ I must think of a

a tempo

new life _____ and I must-n't give in. _____ When the

dawn comes to-night will be a mem-o-ry too _____ and a

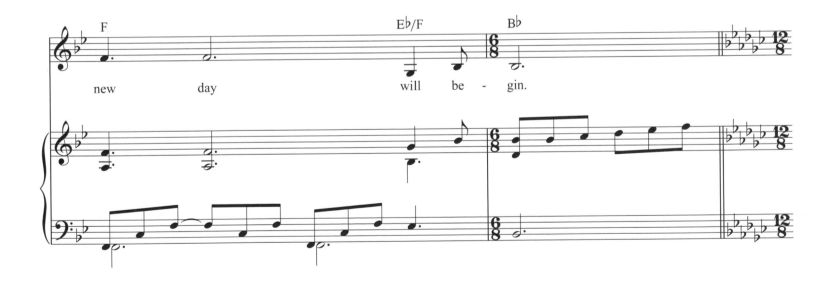

new day will be - gin.

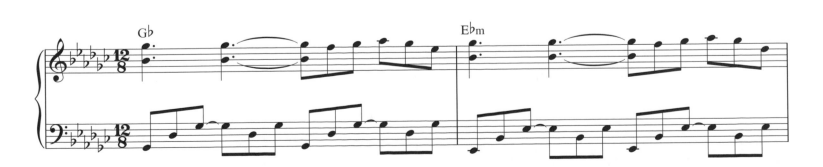

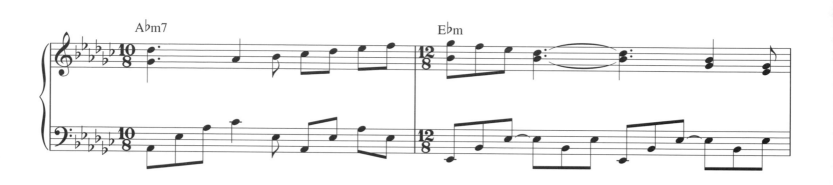

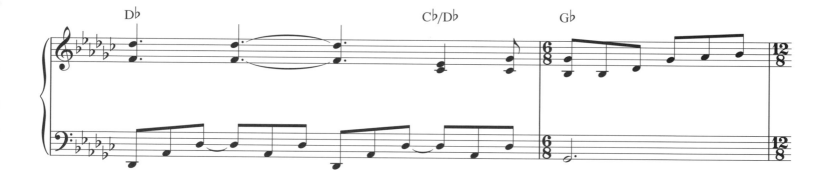

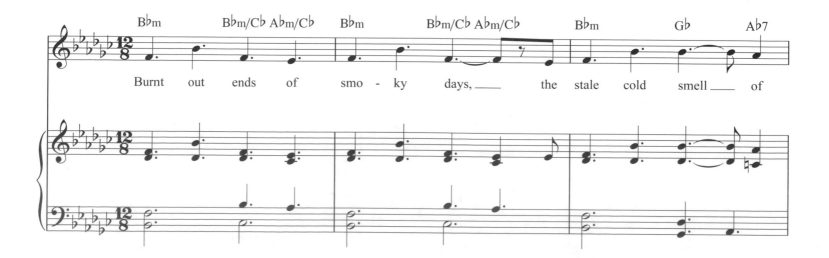

Burnt out ends of smo - ky days, ___ the stale cold smell ___ of

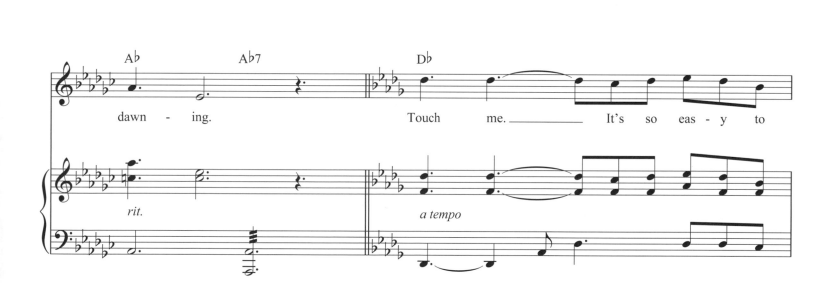

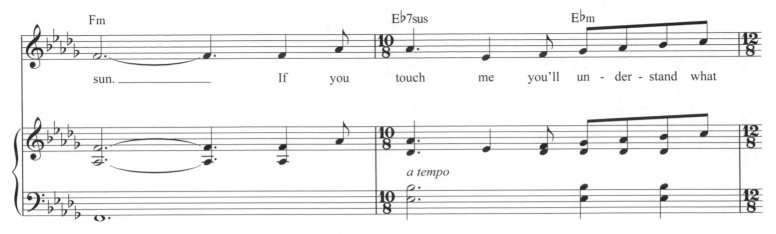

sun. _____ If you touch me you'll un - der - stand what

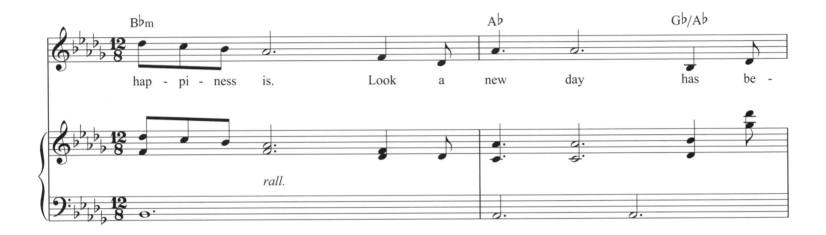

hap - pi - ness is. Look a new day has be -

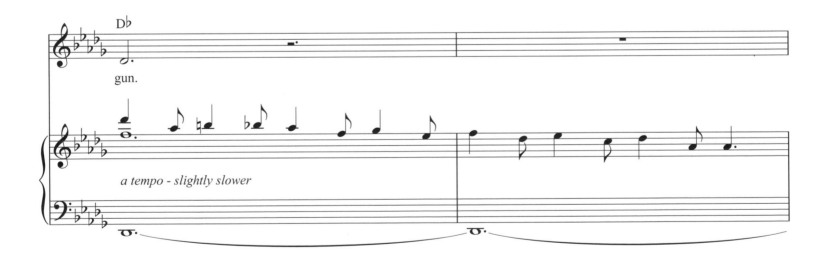

gun.

NO ONE IS ALONE

from INTO THE WOODS

Words and Music by
STEPHEN SONDHEIM

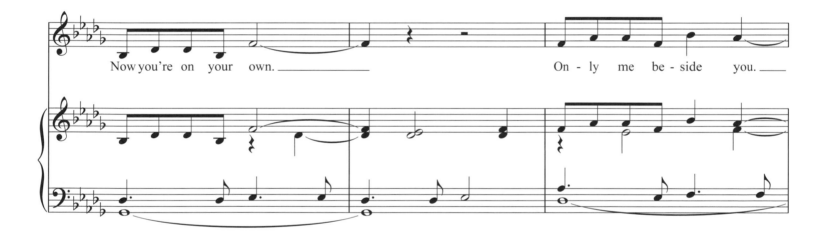

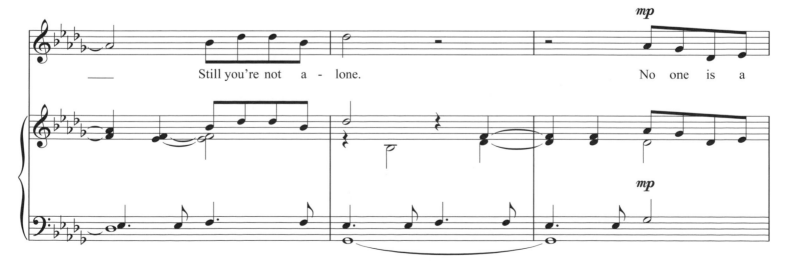

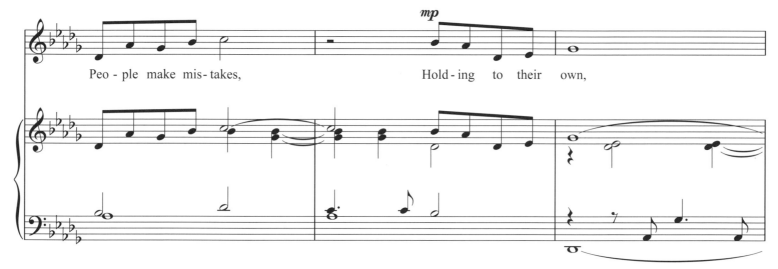

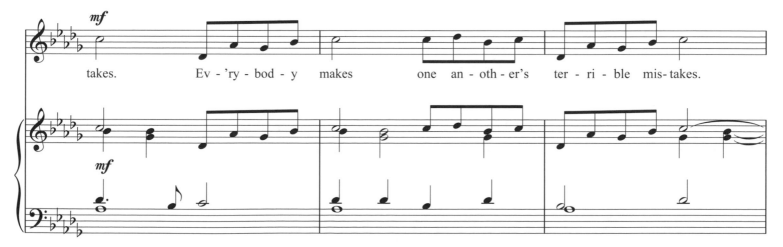

Witch-es can be right, Gi-ants can be good. You de-cide what's

right, You de-cide what's good. Just re-mem-ber: Some-one is on your side. ___

___ Some-one else is not. While you're see-ing your side, ___

___ May-be you for-got: They are not a - lone.

No one is a - lone.

Poco meno mosso

Hard to see the light now. _____ Just don't let it go. _____

Things will come out right now. _____ We can make it so. Someone is on

your side, _____ No one is a - lone. _____

MY FAVORITE THINGS

from THE SOUND OF MUSIC

Lyrics by OSCAR HAMMERSTEIN II
Music by RICHARD RODGERS

Allegro animato

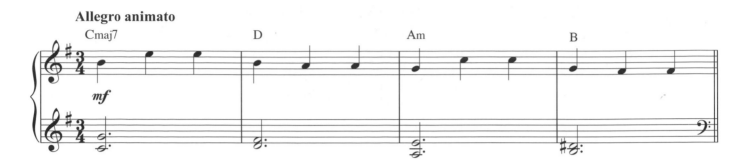

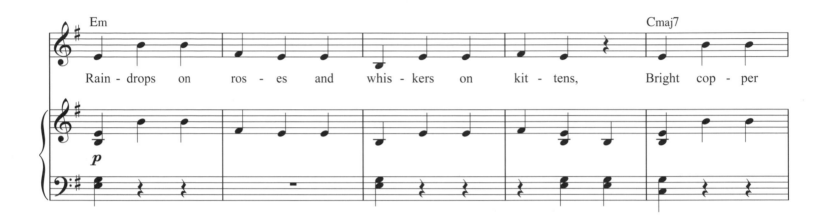

Rain - drops on ros - es and whis - kers on kit - tens, Bright cop - per

ket - tles and warm wool - en mit - tens, Brown pa - per pack - ag - es

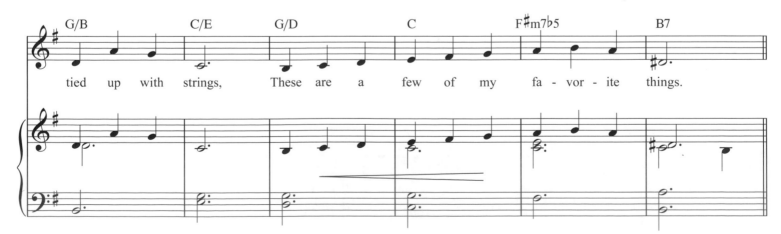

tied up with strings, These are a few of my fa - vor - ite things.

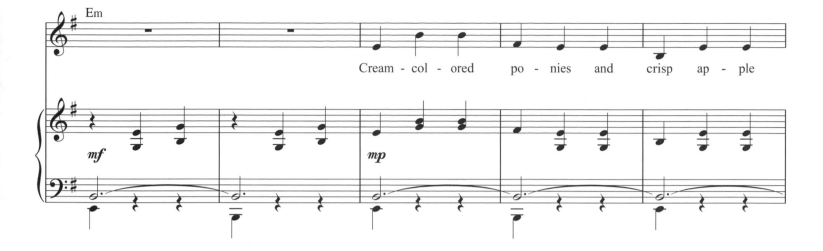

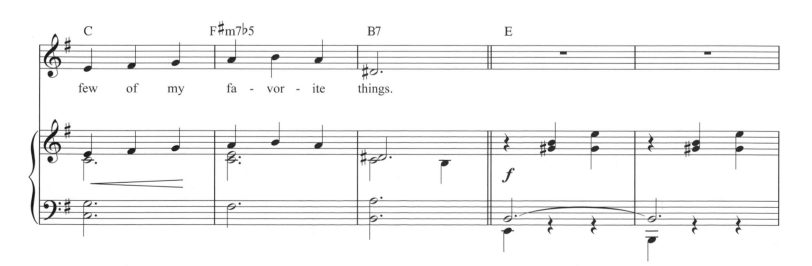

Girls in white dress - es with blue sat - in sash - es, Snow - flakes that stay on my nose and eye - lash - es, Sil - ver white win - ters that melt in - to springs, These are a few of my fa - vor - ite things.

When the dog bites, When the bee stings, When I'm

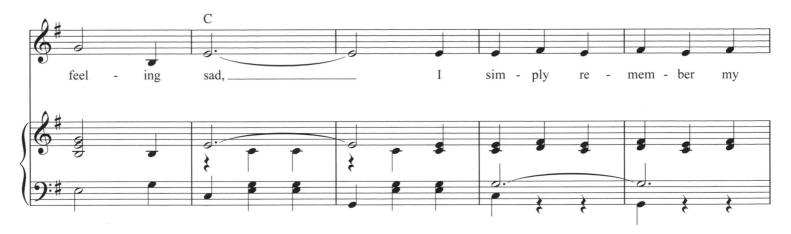

feel - ing sad, _____ I sim - ply re - mem - ber my

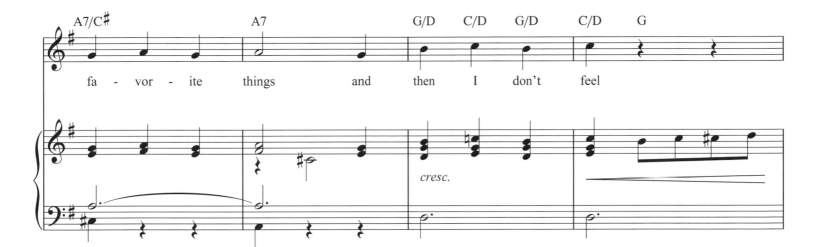

fa - vor - ite things and then I don't feel

cresc.

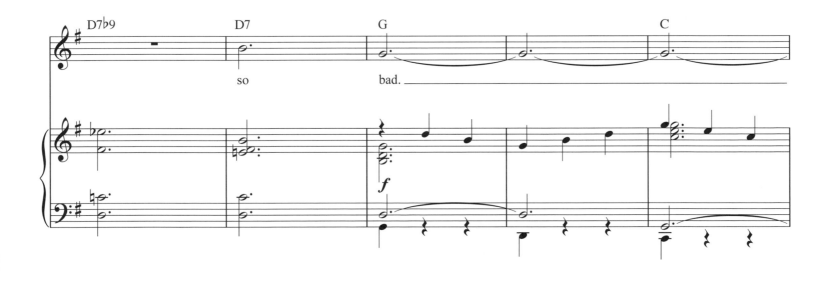

so bad. _____

f

sf

8vb

MY FUNNY VALENTINE

from BABES IN ARMS

Words by LORENZ HART
Music by RICHARD RODGERS

tent. Thou no - ble, up - right, truth - ful, sin - cere and slight - ly dop - ey

Slowly, with much expression

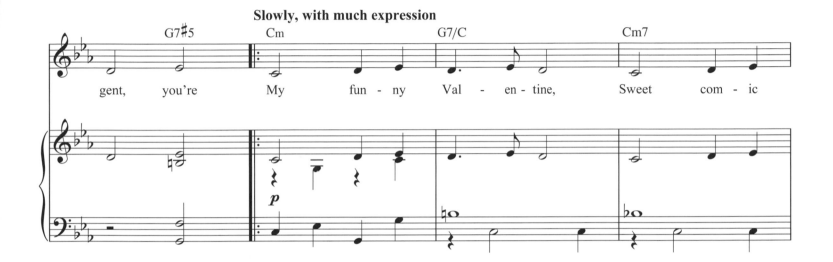

gent, you're My fun - ny Val - en - tine, Sweet com - ic

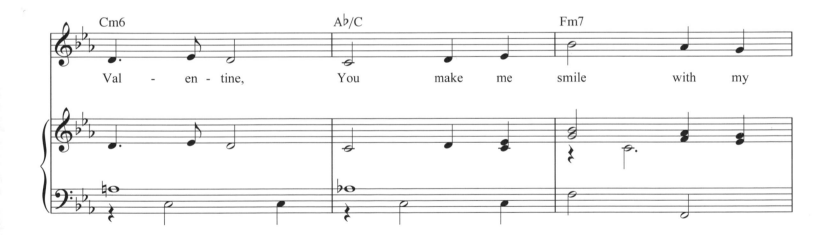

Val - en - tine, You make me smile with my

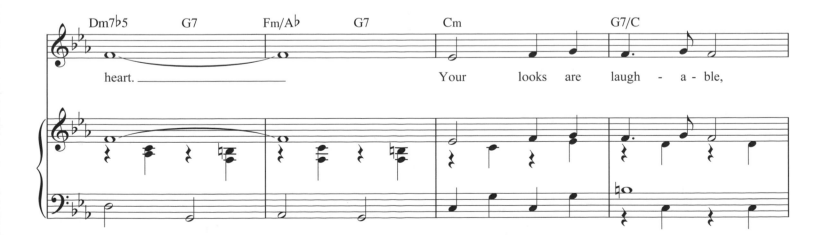

heart. _____ Your looks are laugh - a - ble,

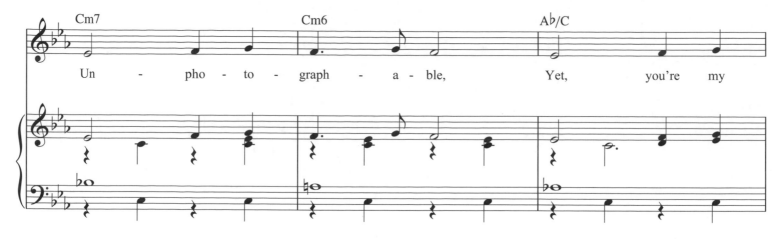

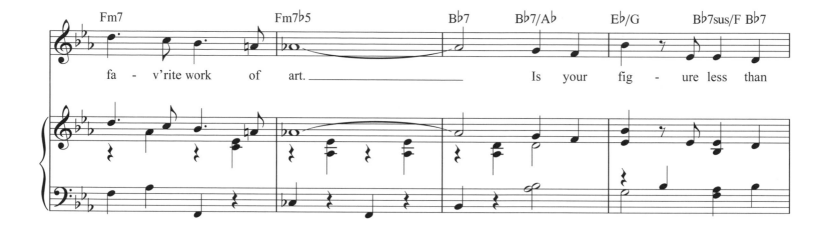

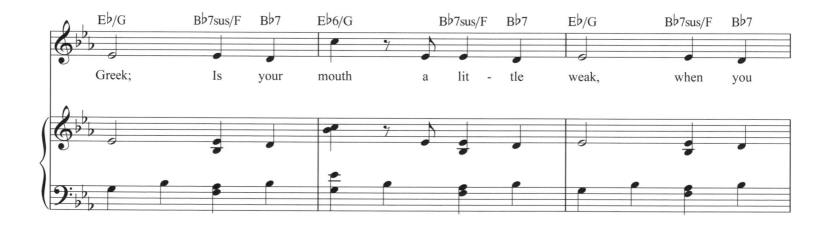

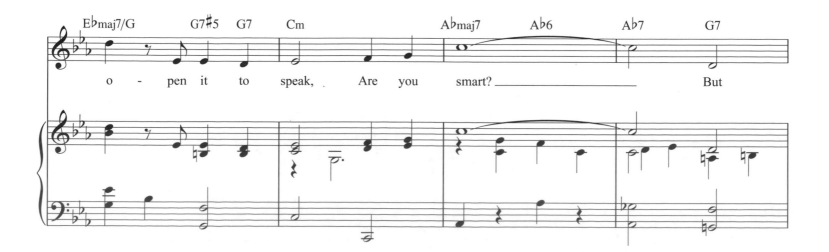

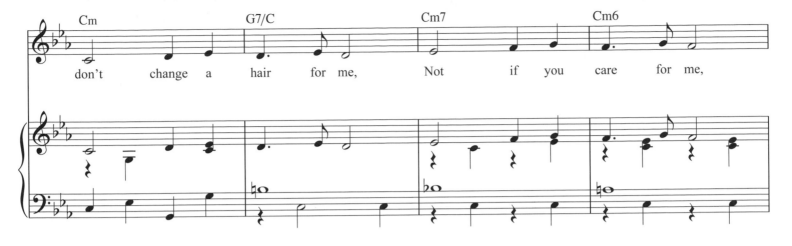

don't change a hair for me, Not if you care for me,

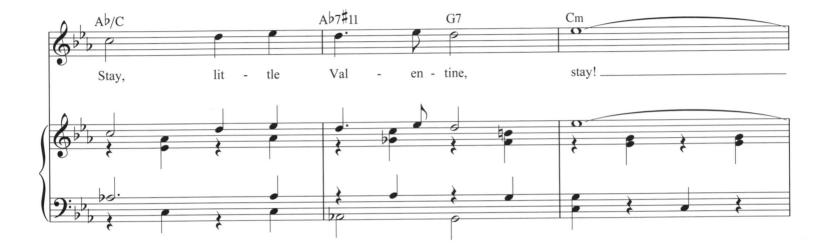

Stay, lit - tle Val - en - tine, stay! _____

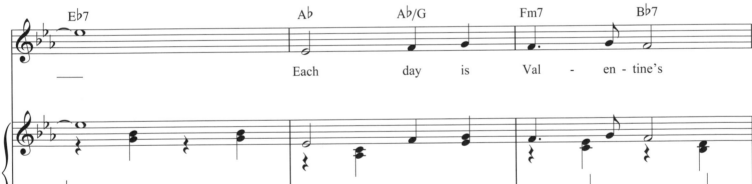

_____ Each day is Val - en - tine's

day. _____   day. _____

OH, WHAT A BEAUTIFUL MORNIN'

from OKLAHOMA!

Lyrics by OSCAR HAMMERSTEIN II
Music by RICHARD RODGERS

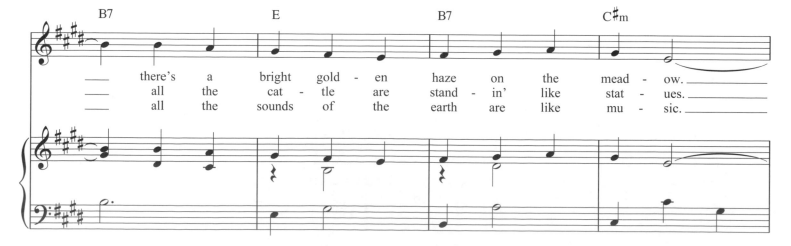

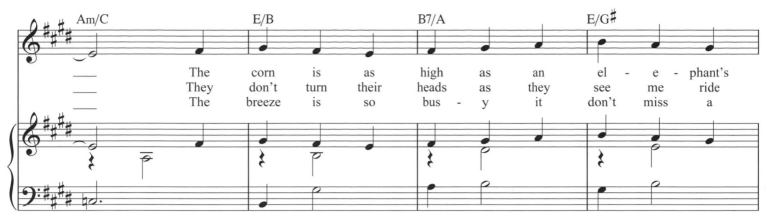

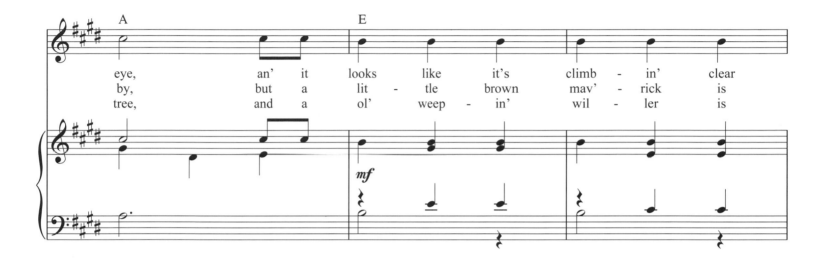

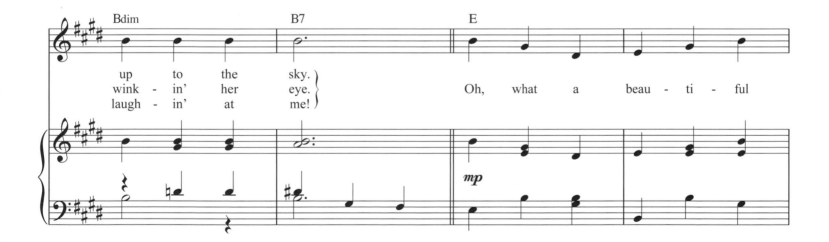

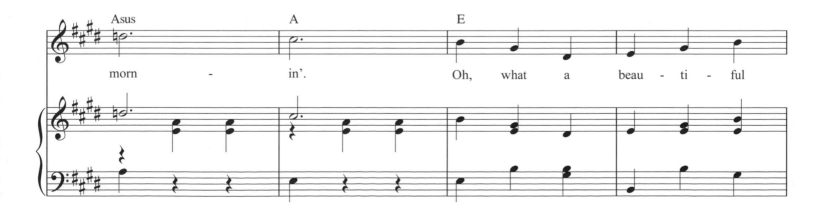

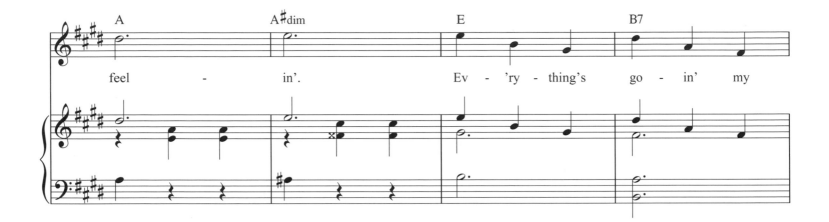

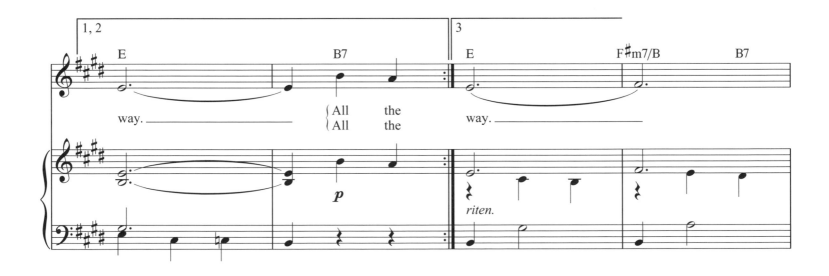

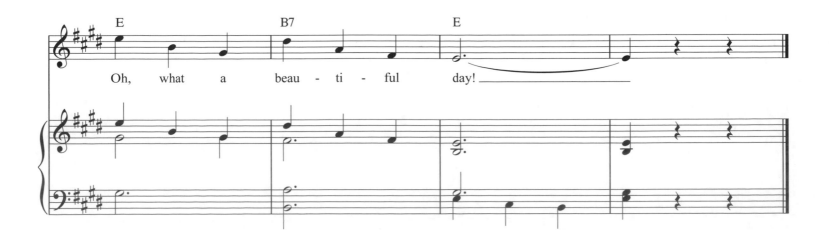

ON THE STREET WHERE YOU LIVE

from MY FAIR LADY

Words by ALAN JAY LERNER
Music by FREDERICK LOEWE

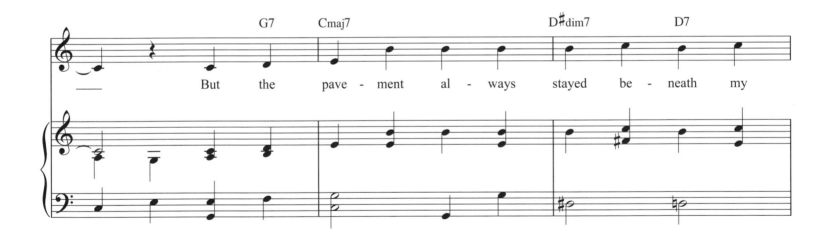

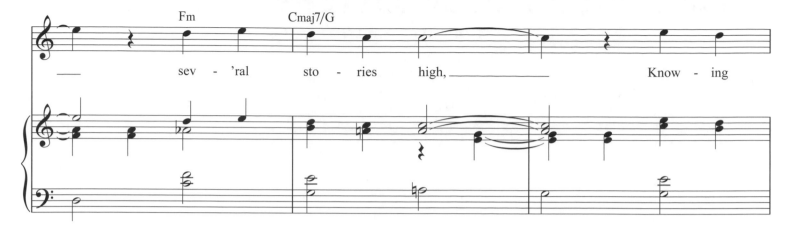

sev - 'ral sto - ries high, _____ Know - ing

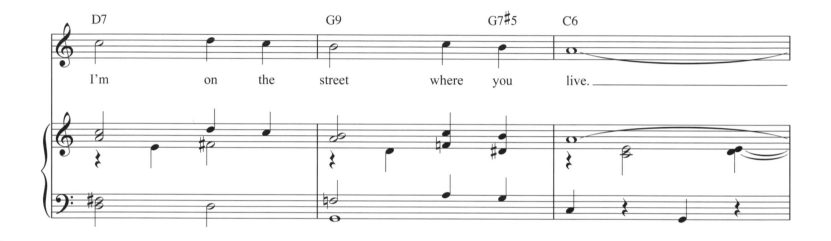

I'm on the street where you live. _____

_____ Are there li - lac trees _____ in the

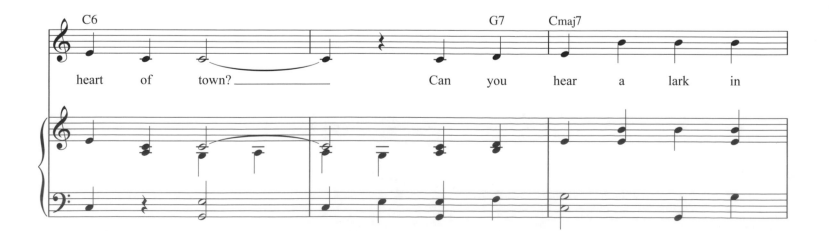

heart of town? _____ Can you hear a lark in

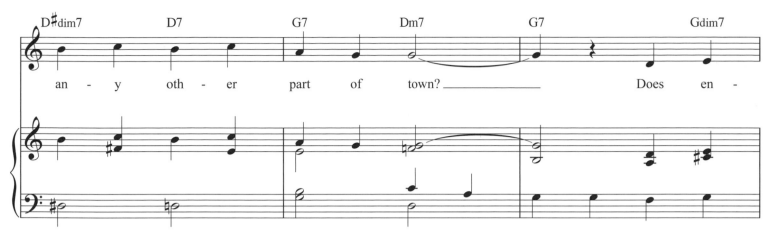

an - y oth - er part of town? _____ Does en -

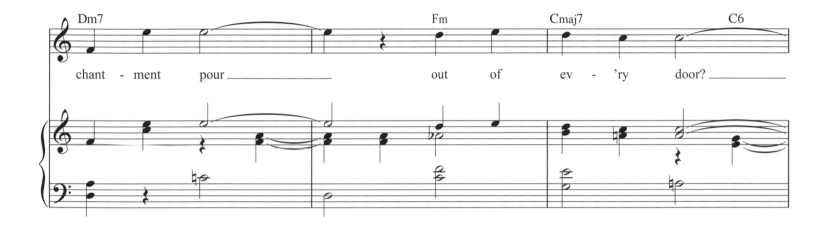

chant - ment pour _____ out of ev - 'ry door? _____

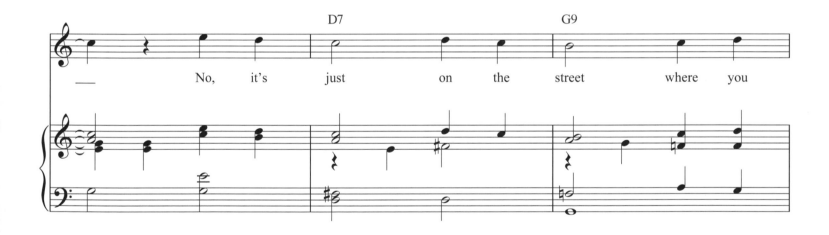

____ No, it's just on the street where you

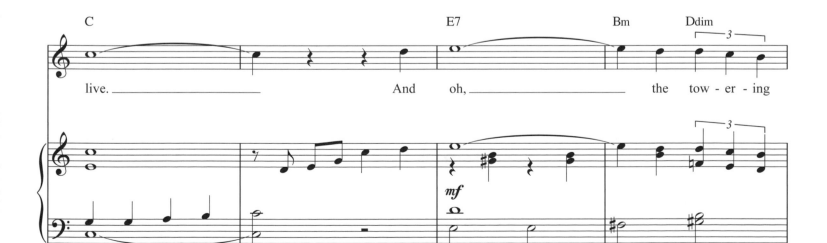

live. _____ And oh, _____ the tow - er - ing

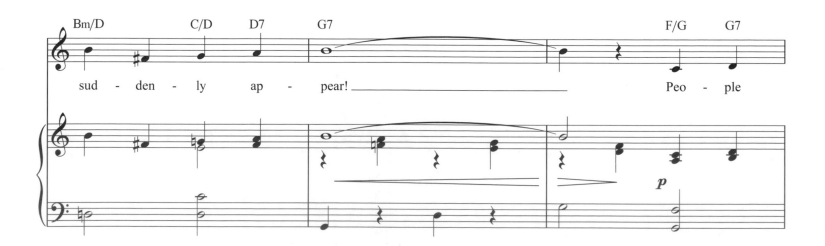

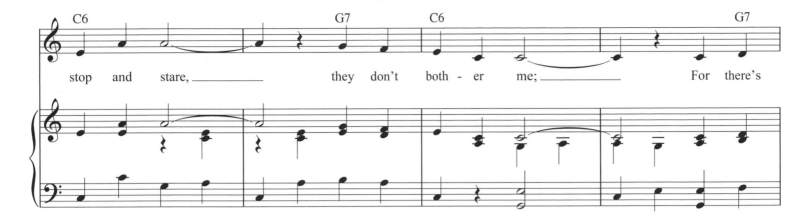

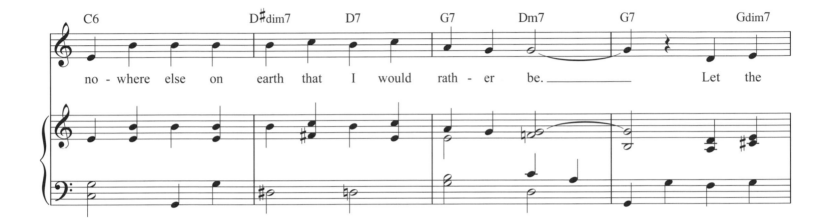

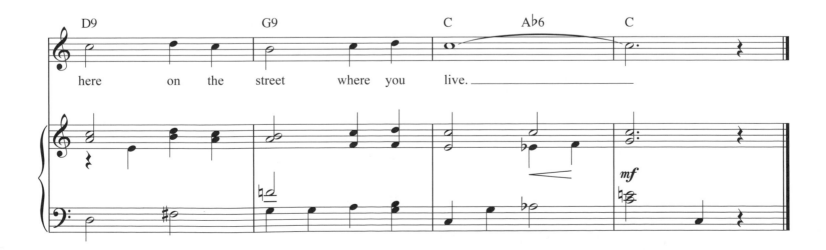

PART OF YOUR WORLD

from THE LITTLE MERMAID - A BROADWAY MUSICAL

Music by ALAN MENKEN
Lyrics by HOWARD ASHMAN

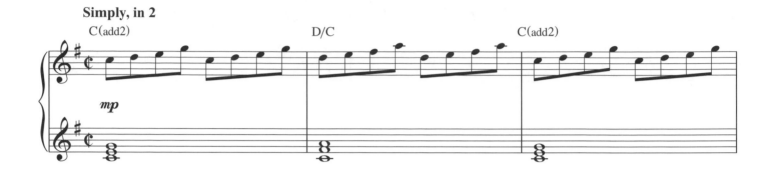

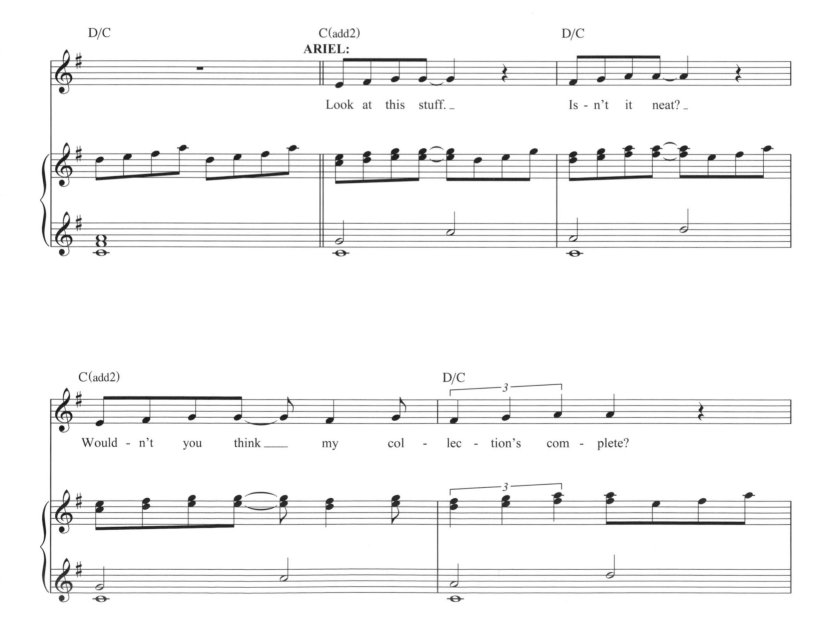

Would-n't you think I'm the girl, the girl who has ev - 'ry - thing?

Look at this trove, treas-ures un - told.

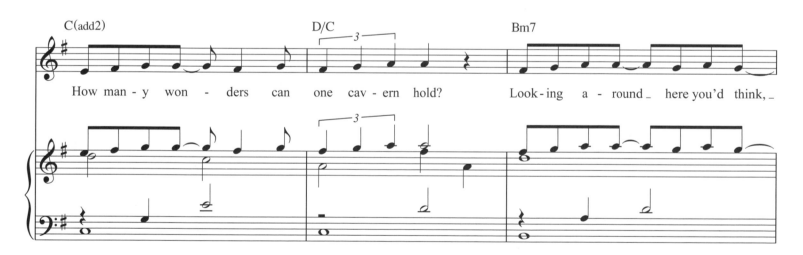

How man - y won - ders can one cav - ern hold? Look-ing a - round here you'd think,

"Sure, she's got ev - 'ry - thing." I've got

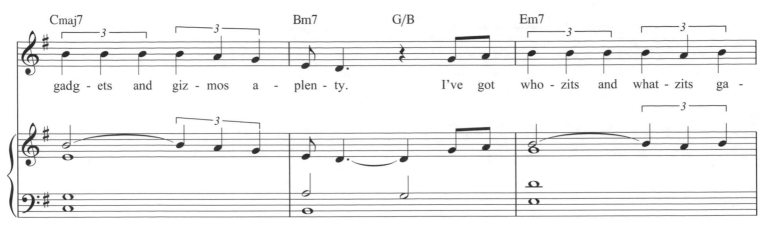

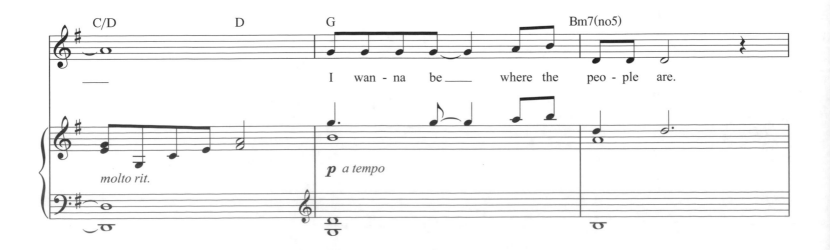

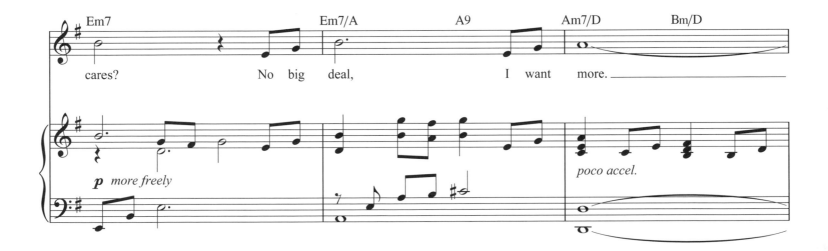

Street. Up where they walk, up where they

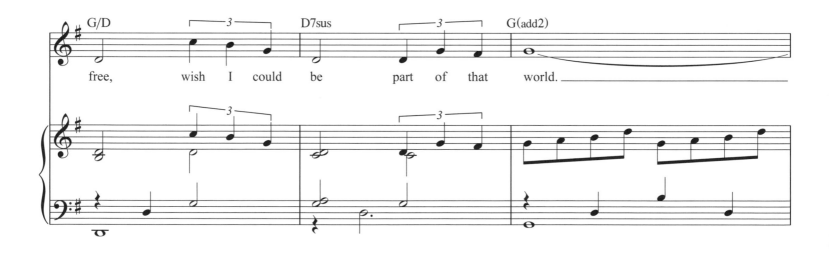

run, up where they stay all day in the sun. Wan - der - in'

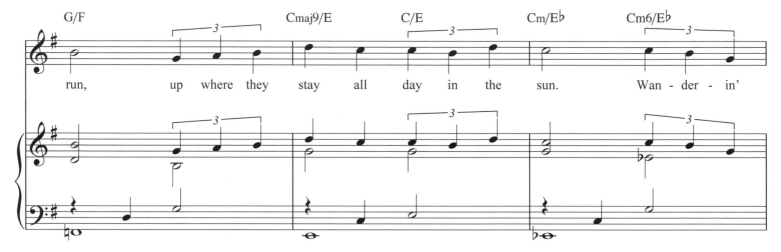

free, wish I could be part of that world. _____

_____ What would I give if I could live out - ta these

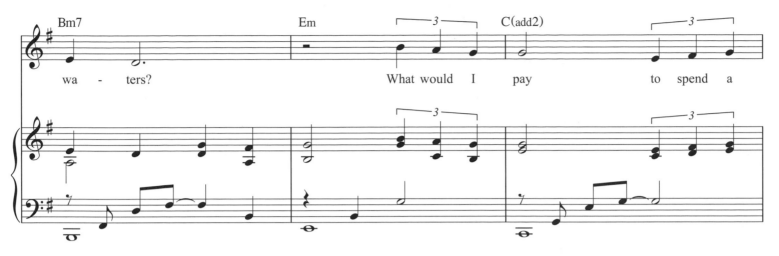

wa - ters? What would I pay to spend a

day warm on the sand? Bet - cha on

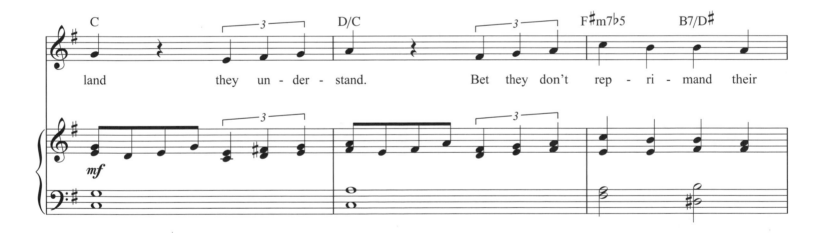

land they un - der - stand. Bet they don't rep - ri - mand their

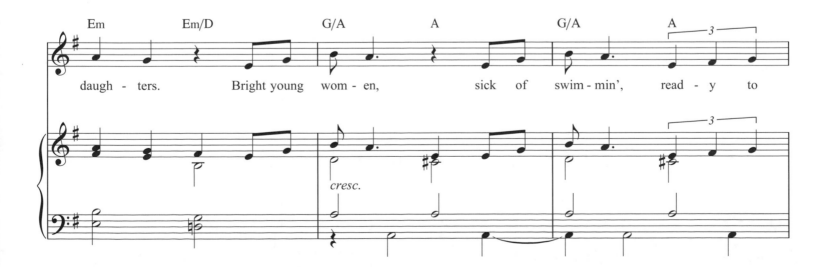

daugh - ters. Bright young wom - en, sick of swim - min', read - y to

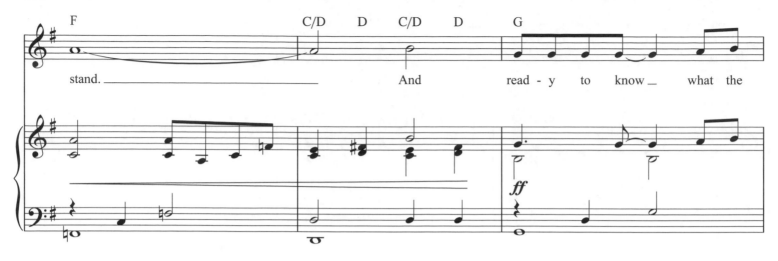

stand._____ And read - y to know _ what the

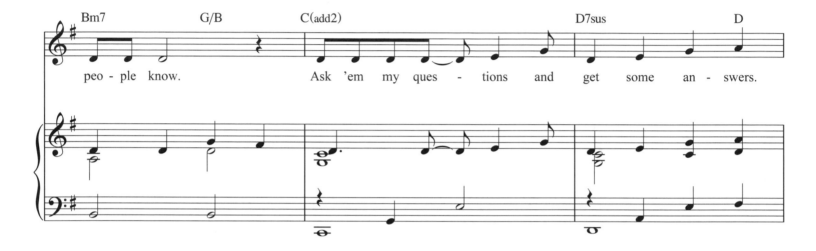

peo - ple know. Ask 'em my ques - tions and get some an - swers.

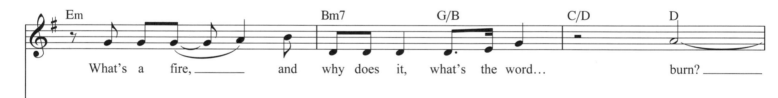

What's a fire, _____ and why does it, what's the word... burn? _____

_____ When's it my turn? Would - n't I love, love to ex -

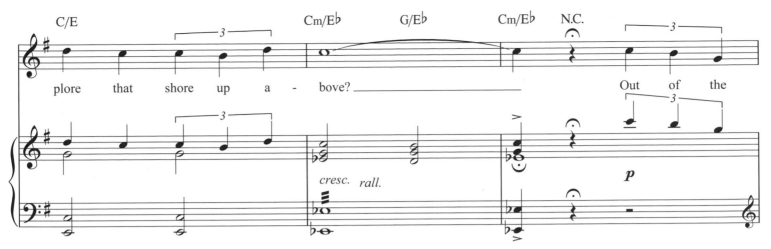

plore that shore up a - bove? _____ Out of the

Freely

sea, _____ wish I could be

part of that world. _____

PEOPLE
from FUNNY GIRL

Words by BOB MERRILL
Music by JULE STYNE

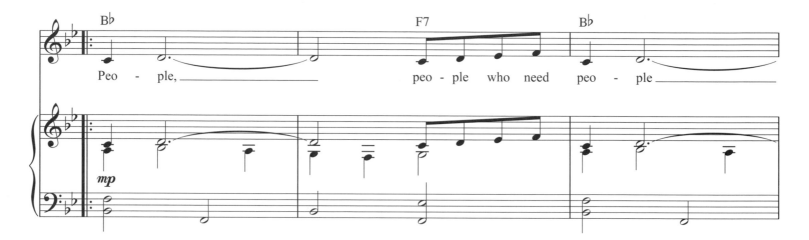

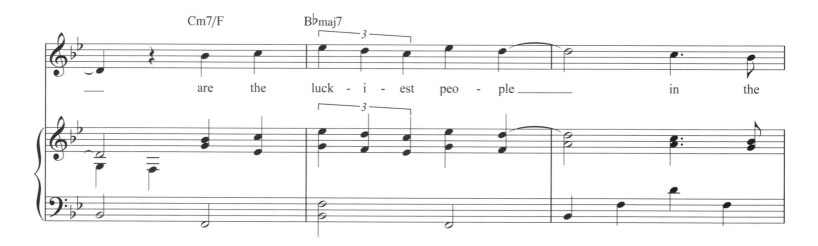

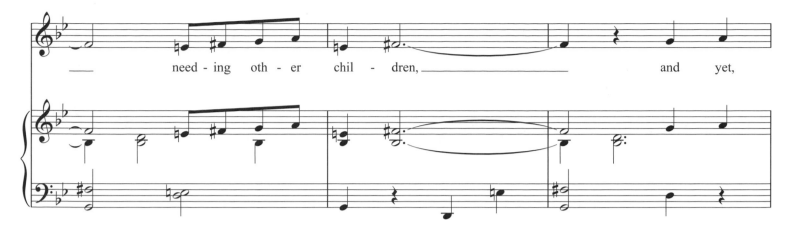

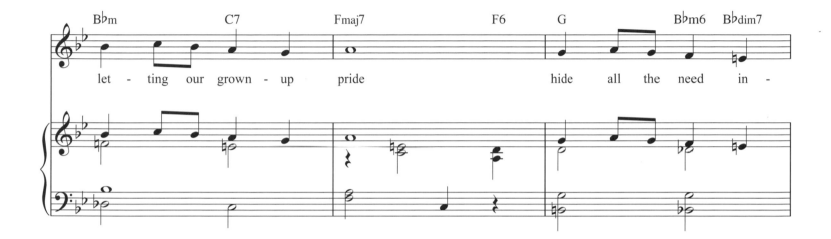

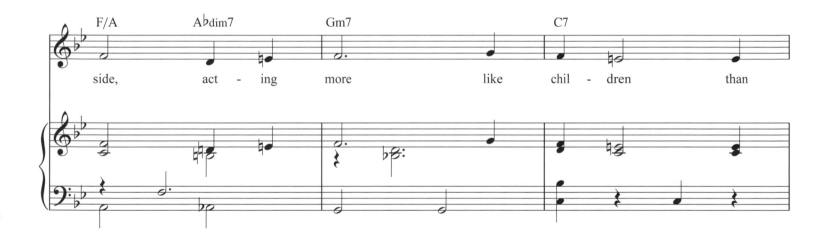

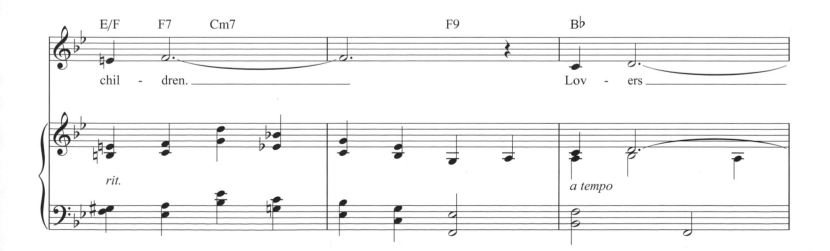

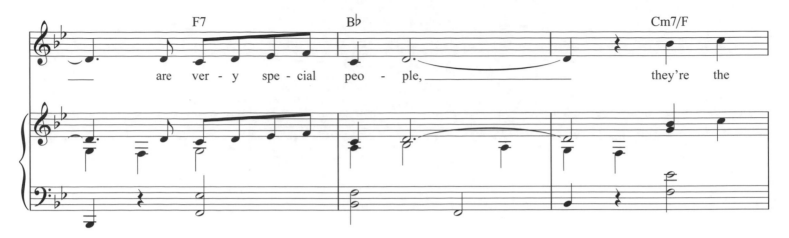

are ver-y spe-cial peo-ple, _____ they're the

luck-i-est peo-ple _____ in the world. _____

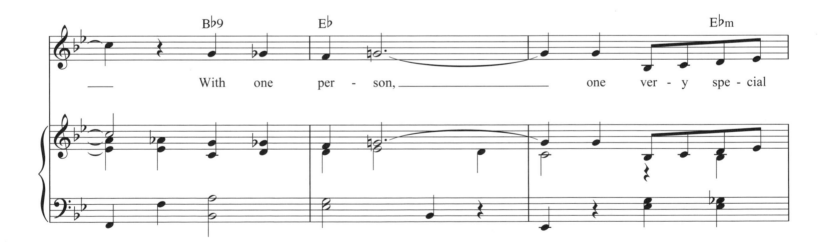

With one per-son, _____ one ver-y spe-cial

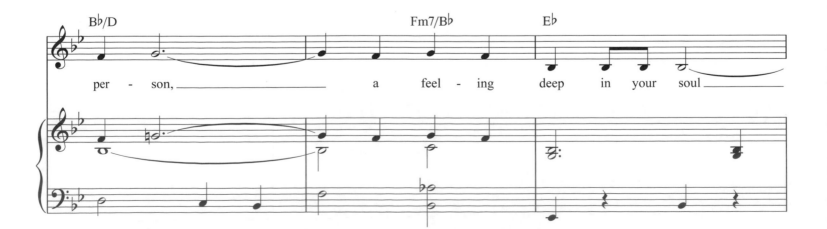

per-son, _____ a feel-ing deep in your soul _____

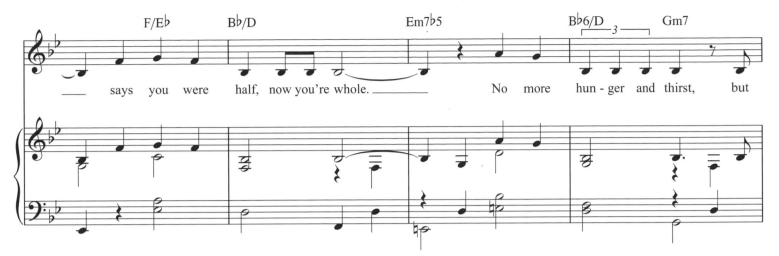

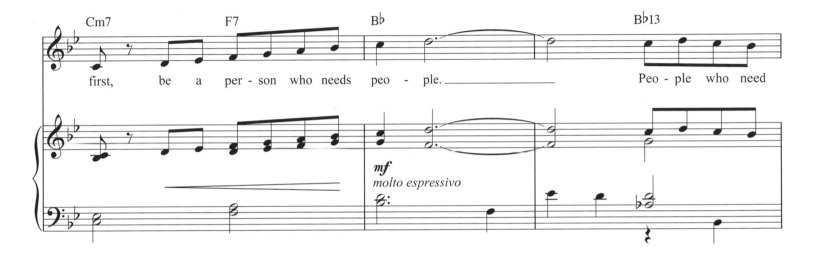

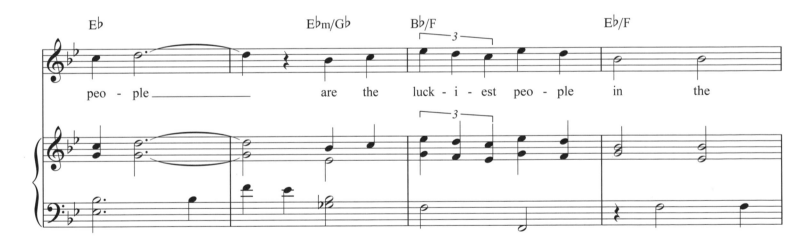

POPULAR
from the Broadway Musical WICKED

Music and Lyrics by
STEPHEN SCHWARTZ

When - ev - er I see some-one less for - tu - nate than I— and let's

face it, who is - n't less for - tu - nate than I? —My ten - der heart tends to start to

bleed And when some-one needs a make - o - ver, I sim - ply have to take o - ver; I

know I know ex - act - ly what they need! And e - ven in your case, tho' it's the

tough - est case I've yet to face,___ don't wor - ry, I'm de - ter - mined to suc -

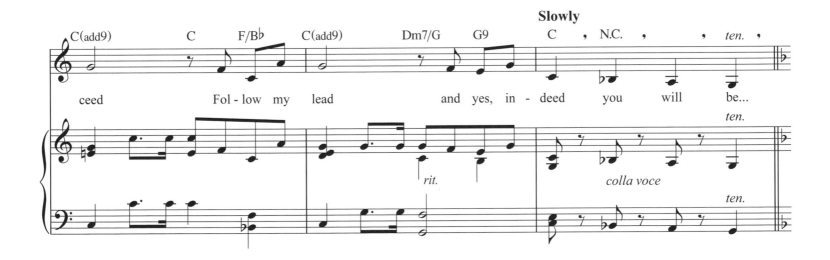

ceed Fol - low my lead and yes, in - deed you will be...

Pop - u - lar,___ You're gon - na be pop - u - lar! I'll teach you the

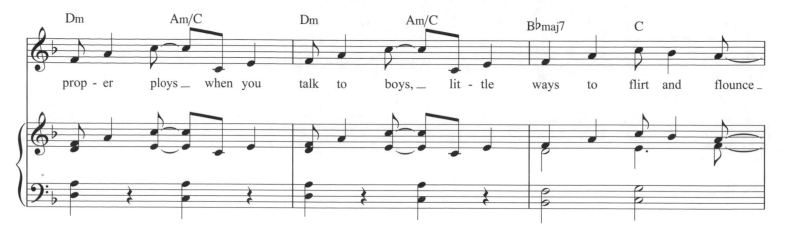

prop - er ploys_ when you talk to boys,_ lit - tle ways to flirt and flounce_

_ I'll show you what shoes to wear, how to fix your hair, _

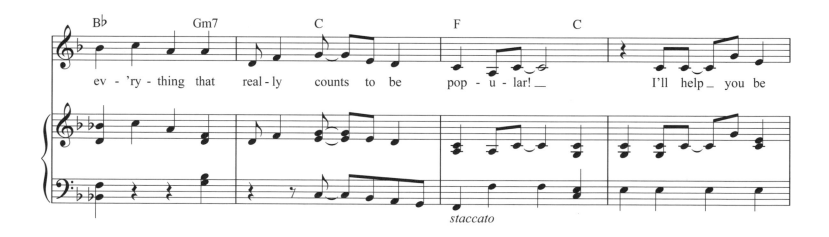

ev - 'ry - thing that real - ly counts to be pop - u - lar! _ I'll help _ you be

staccato

pop - u - lar! You'll hang _ with the right co - horts, _ you'll be

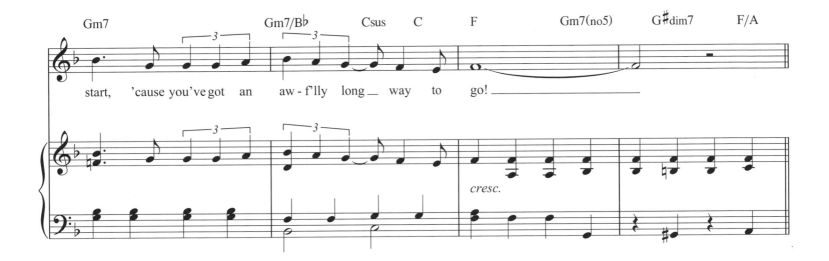

be - com - ing pop - u - ler... lar... _____

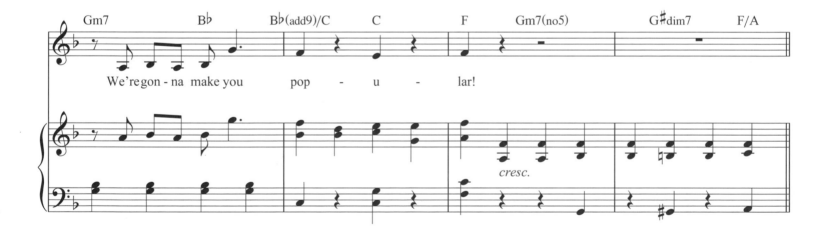

La la _____ la la _____

We're gon - na make you pop - u - lar!

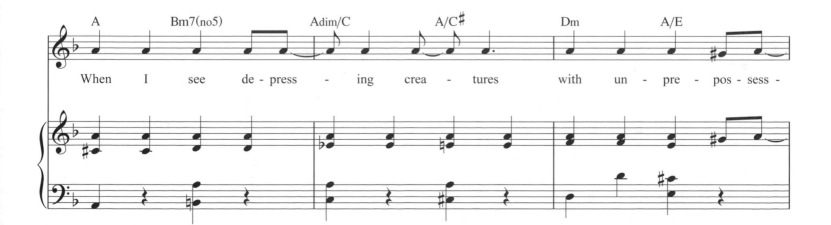

When I see de - press - ing crea - tures with un - pre - pos - sess -

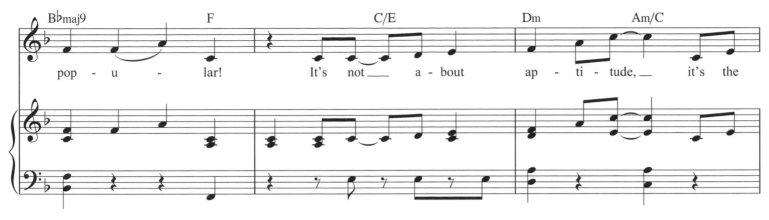

pop - u - lar! It's not _ a - bout ap - ti - tude, _ it's the

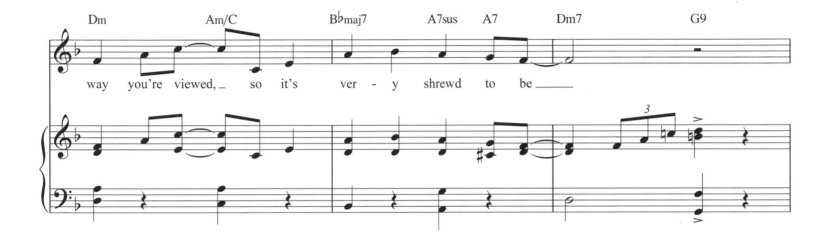

way you're viewed, _ so it's ver - y shrewd to be _____

ver - y, ver - y pop - u - lar like me! And tho'

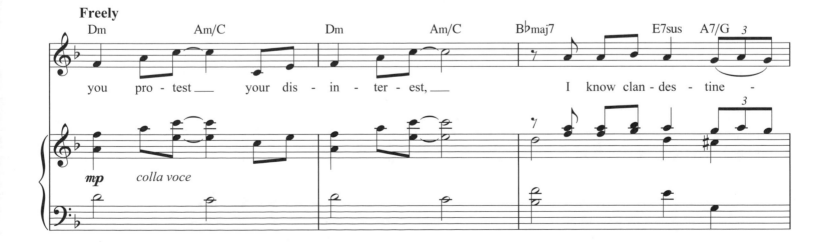

you pro - test _ your dis - in - ter - est, _ I know clan - des - tine -

172

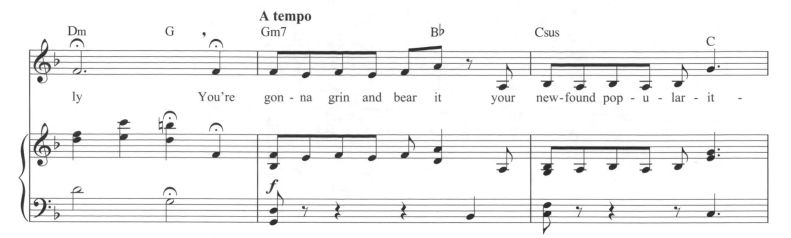

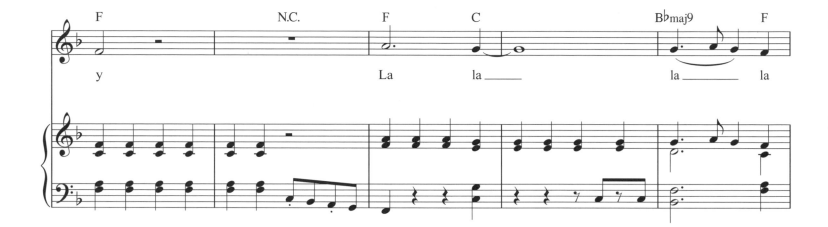

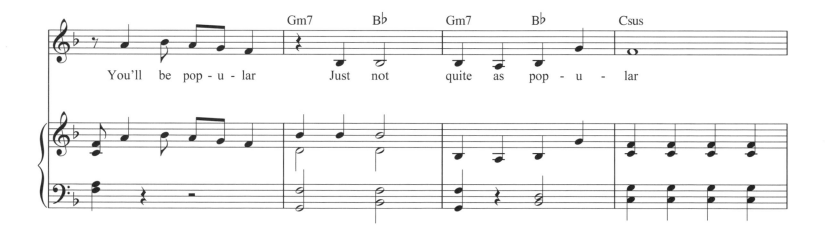

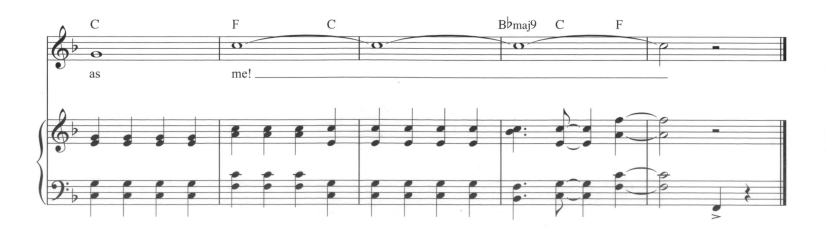

PUT ON A HAPPY FACE
from BYE BYE BIRDIE

Lyric by LEE ADAMS
Music by CHARLES STROUSE

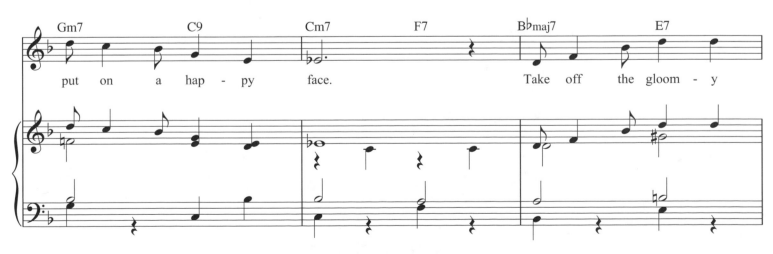

mask of trag - e - dy, it's not your style;

You'll look so good that you'll be glad ___ ya' de - cid - ed to smile! ___

___ Pick out a pleas - ant out - look, ___

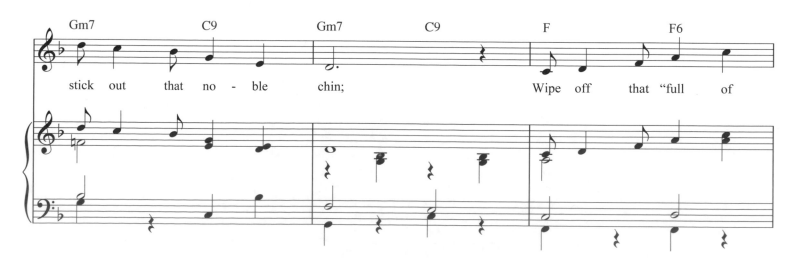

stick out that no - ble chin; Wipe off that "full of

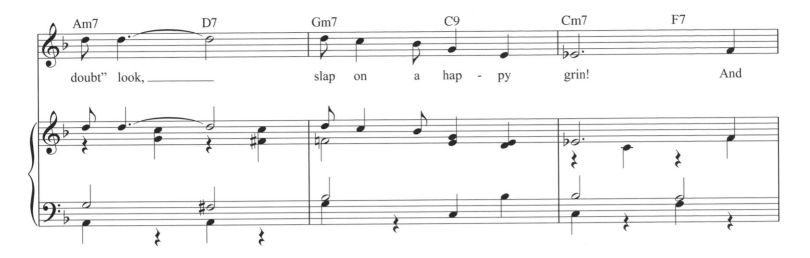

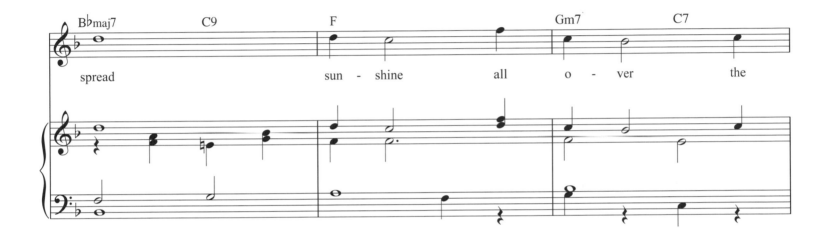

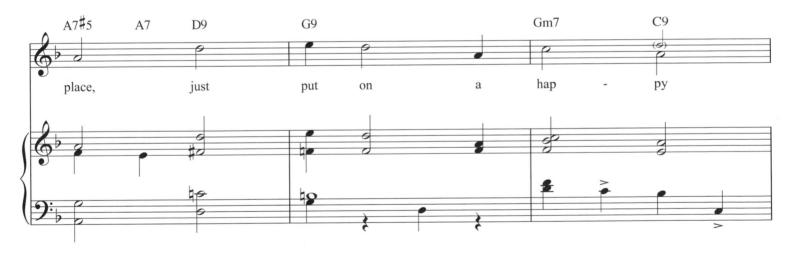

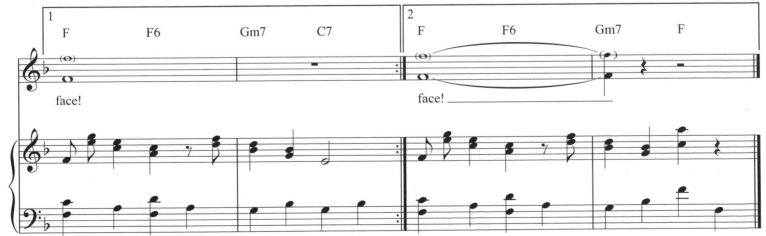

Send in the Clowns
from the Musical A LITTLE NIGHT MUSIC

Words and Music by
STEPHEN SONDHEIM

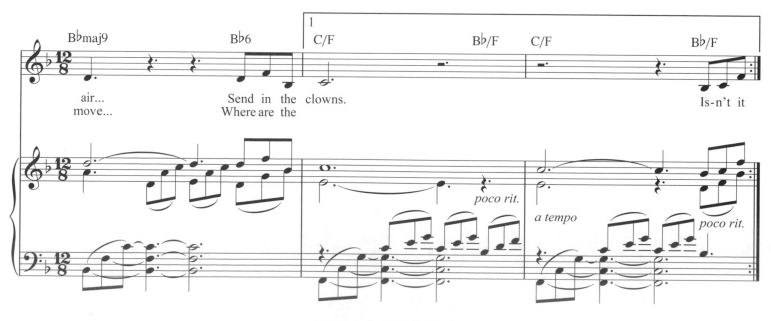

clowns?　　Send in the clowns.　　Just when I'd

stopped
prise!　　　o - pen - ing doors,　　Fi - nal - ly
　　　　　Who could fore - see　　　I'd come to

know-ing the one that I want-ed was　yours,　　Mak - ing my
feel a - bout you what you feel a - bout　me?　　Why on - ly

en - trance a - gain with my u - su - al　flair,　　Sure of my lines,　　No one is
now when I see that you've drift-ed a - way?　　What a sur - prise...　　What a cli-

SOME ENCHANTED EVENING

from SOUTH PACIFIC

Lyrics by OSCAR HAMMERSTEIN II
Music by RICHARD RODGERS

Moderato

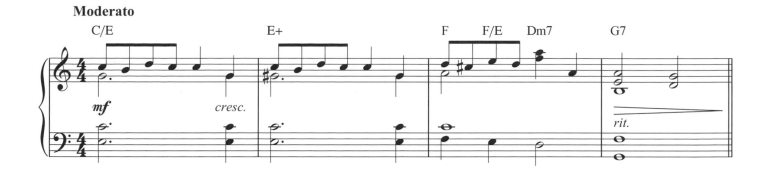

Some en-chant-ed eve-ning _____ you may see a stran-ger, _____

you may see a stran-ger _____ a-cross a

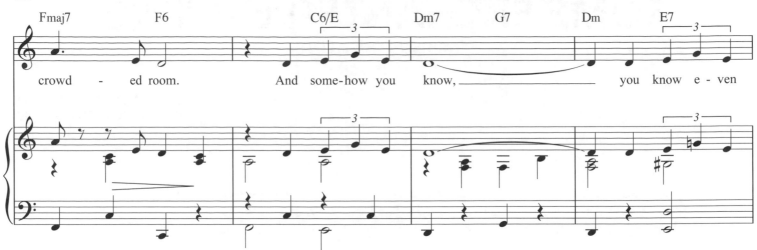

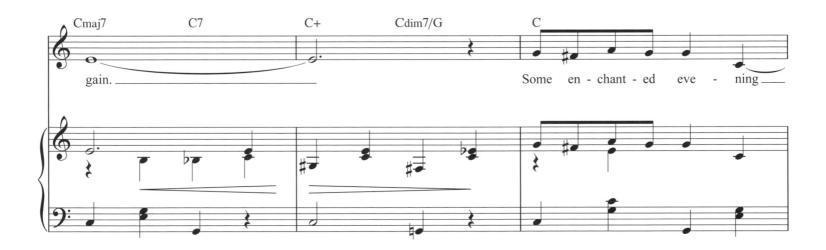

you may hear her laugh - ing _____ a - cross a crowd - ed room.

And night af - ter night, _____ as strange as it seems, _____

_____ the sound of her laugh - ter will sing in your dreams. _____

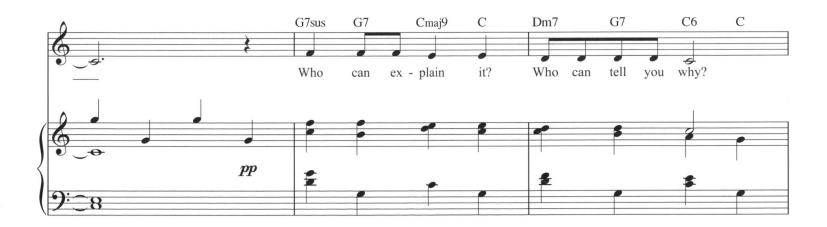

Who can ex - plain it? Who can tell you why?

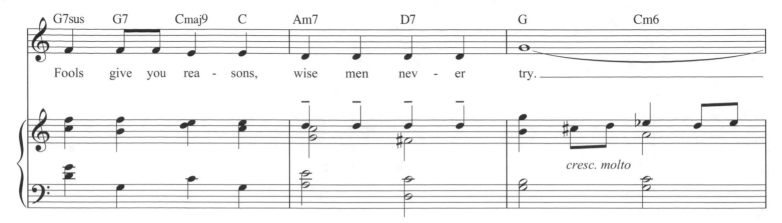

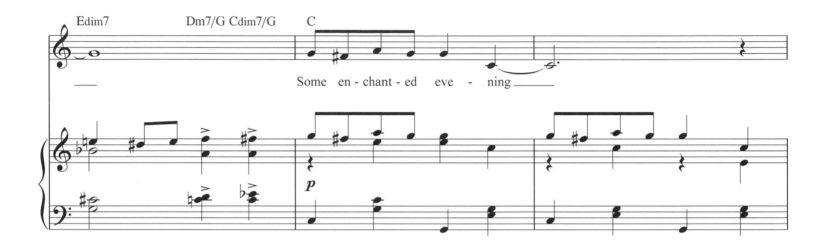

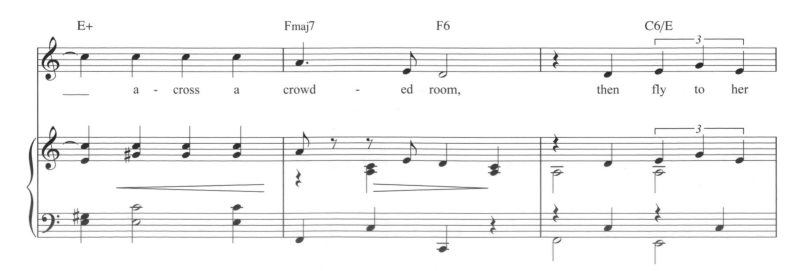

SHY
from ONCE UPON A MATTRESS

Words by MARSHALL BARER
Music by MARY RODGERS

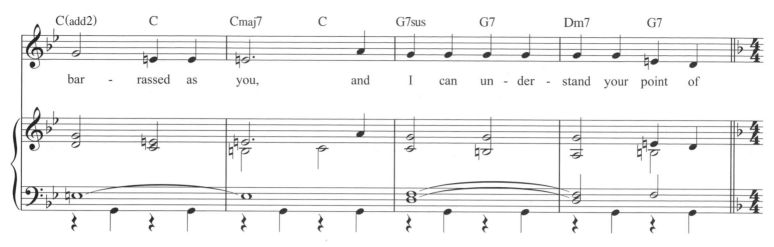

bar - rassed as you, and I can un - der - stand your point of

Moderato

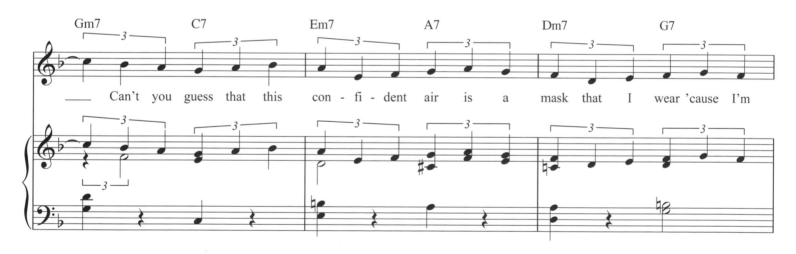

view? I've al - ways been shy, _____ I con - fess it, I'm shy. _____

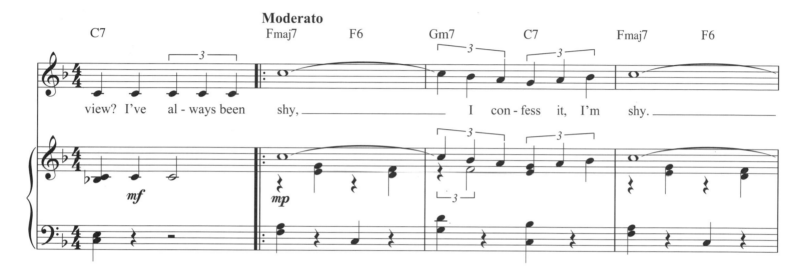

_____ Can't you guess that this con - fi - dent air is a mask that I wear 'cause I'm

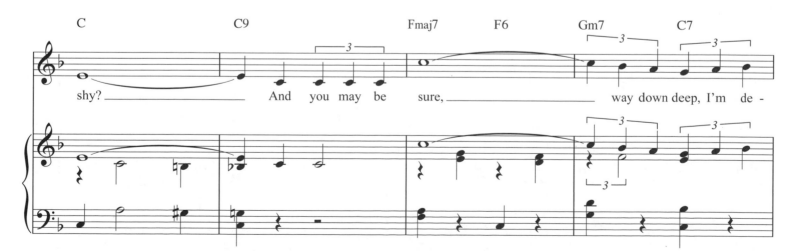

shy? _____ And you may be sure, _____ way down deep, I'm de -

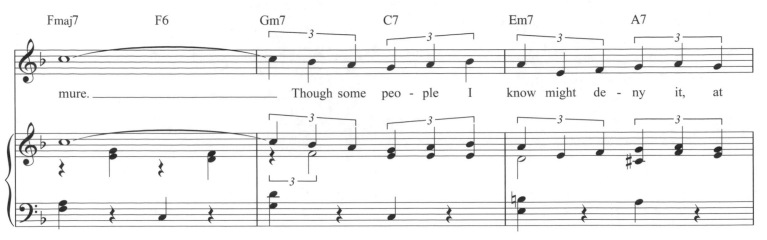

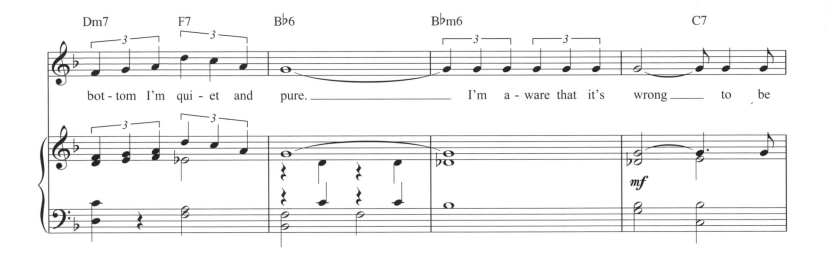

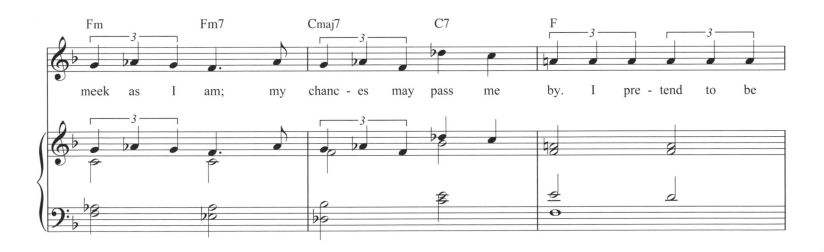

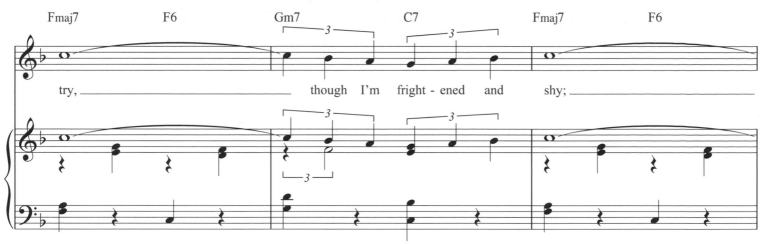

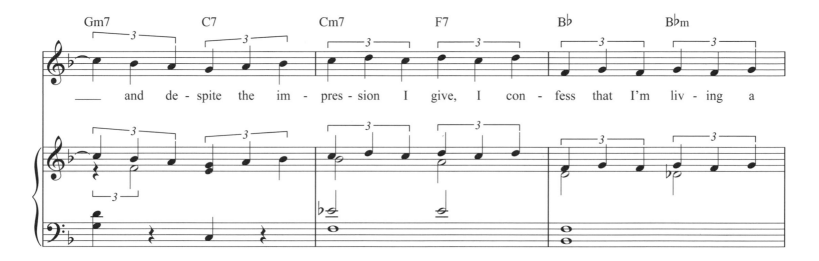

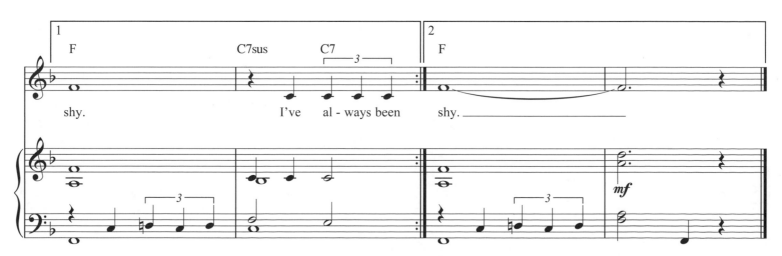

SOMEONE TO WATCH OVER ME

from OH, KAY!

Music and Lyrics by GEORGE GERSHWIN
and IRA GERSHWIN

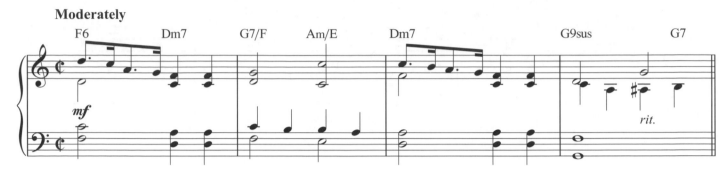

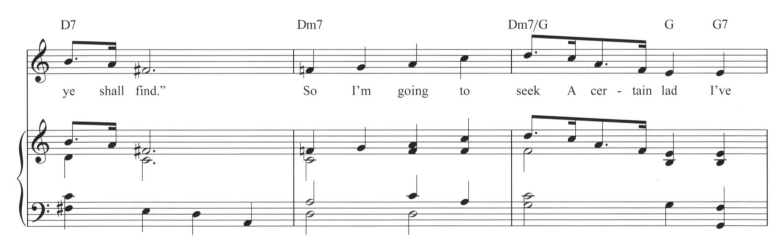

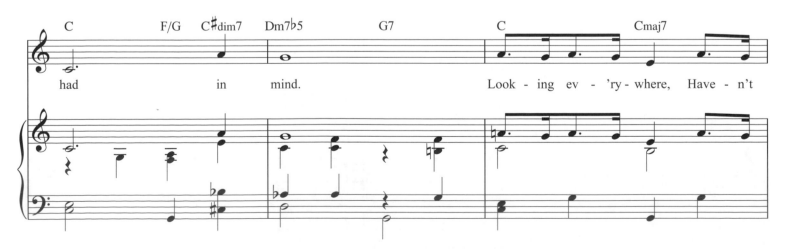

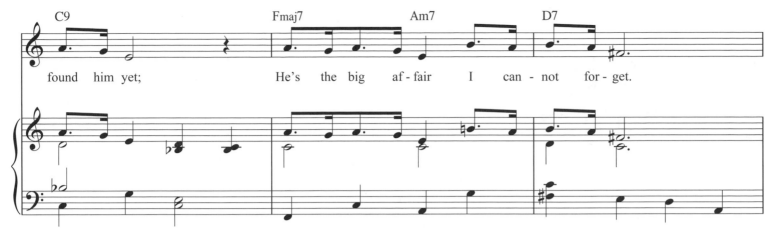

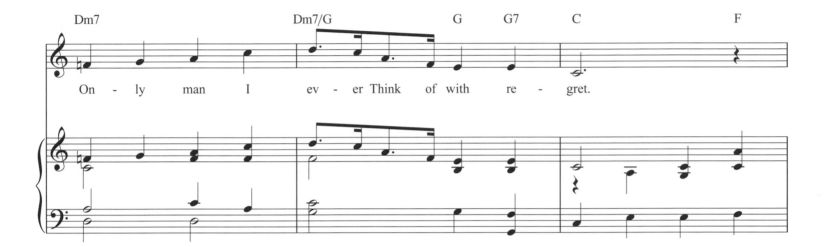

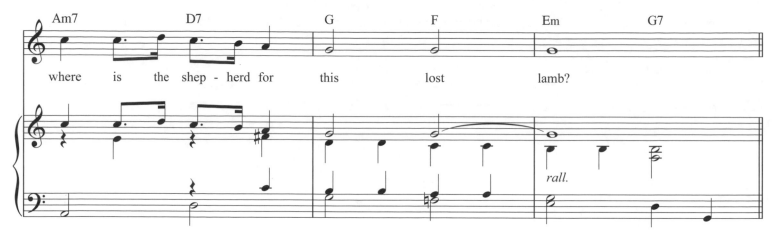

where is the shep - herd for this lost lamb?

There's a some-bod - y I'm long - ing to see. I hope that he

Turns out to be Some - one who'll watch o - ver

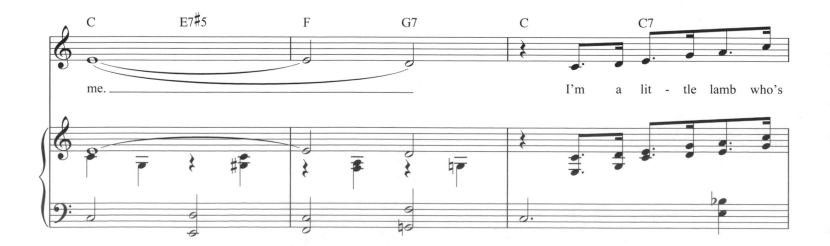

me. _____ I'm a lit - tle lamb who's

191

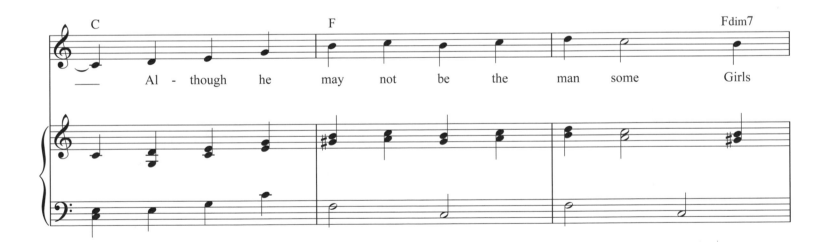

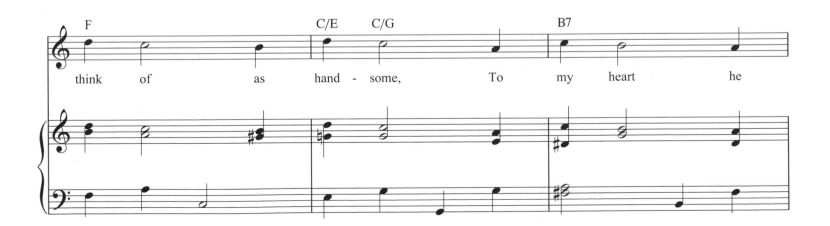

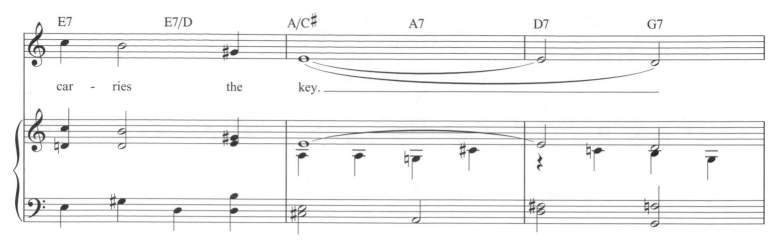

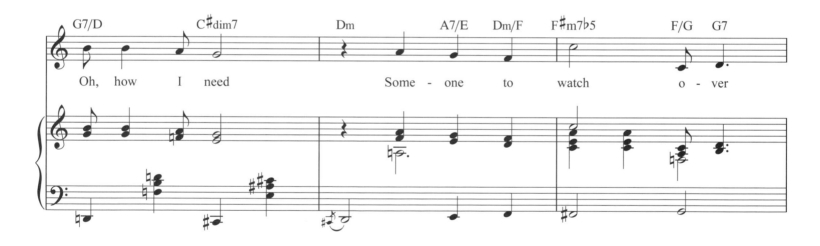

THE SOUND OF MUSIC

from THE SOUND OF MUSIC

Lyrics by OSCAR HAMMERSTEIN II
Music by RICHARD RODGERS

Molto moderato *(tenderly)*

My day in the hills has come to an end, I know. A star has come out to tell me it's time to go. But deep in the dark green shad-ows are voic-es that urge me to

The hills fill my heart with the sound of mu - sic.

My heart wants to sing ev - 'ry song it hears.

My heart wants to beat like the wings of the birds that rise from the

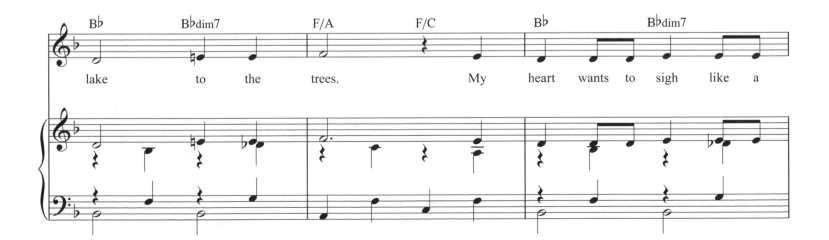

lake to the trees. My heart wants to sigh like a

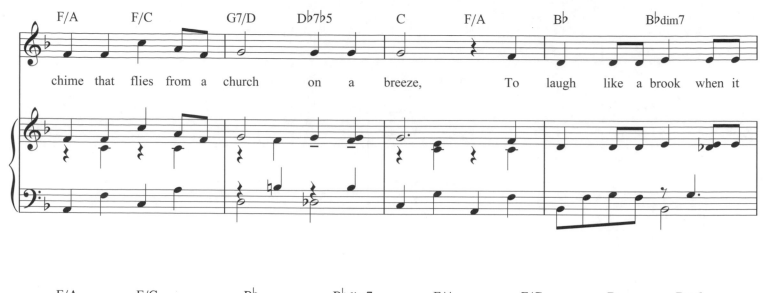

chime that flies from a church on a breeze, To laugh like a brook when it

trips and falls o - ver stones in its way, To sing through the

night like a lark who is learn - ing to pray. I

go to the hills when my heart is lone - ly. I

know I will hear what I've heard be - fore.____

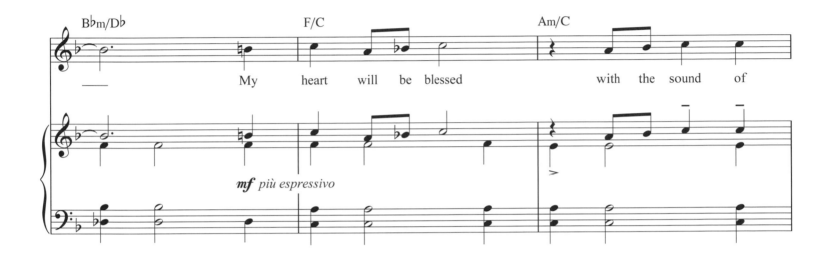

____ My heart will be blessed with the sound of

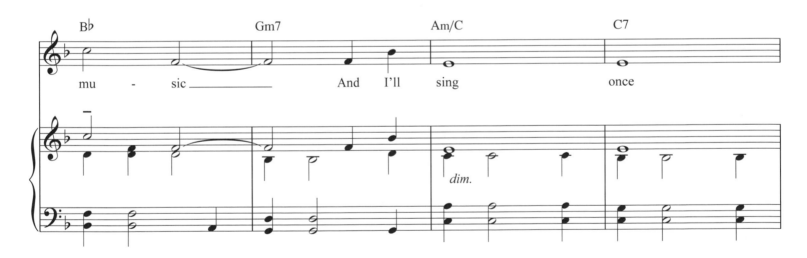

mu - sic____ And I'll sing once

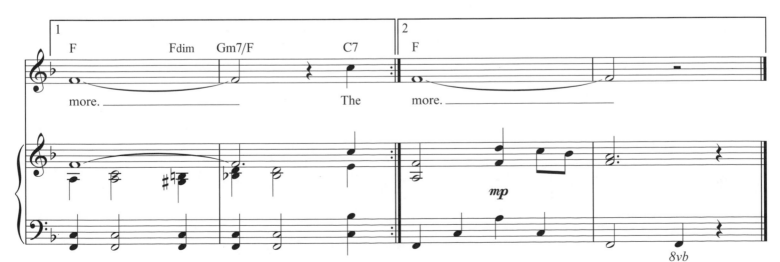

more.____ The more.____

THERE'S NO BUSINESS LIKE SHOW BUSINESS

from the Stage Production ANNIE GET YOUR GUN

Words and Music by
IRVING BERLIN

butch - er, the bak - er, the gro - cer, the clerk get
head - aches, the heart - aches, the back - aches, the flops, the
mu - sic, the mu - sic, the spot - light, the towns, your

paid for what they do but no ap - plause. _____ They'd
sher - iff who es - corts you out of town. _____ The
bag - gage with the la - bels past - ed on. _____ The

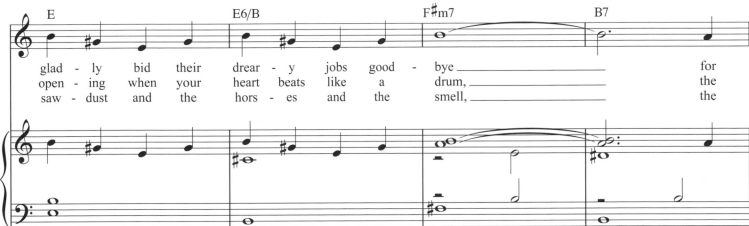

glad - ly bid their drear - y jobs good - bye _____ for
open - ing when your heart beats like a drum, _____ the
saw - dust and the hors - es and the smell, _____ the

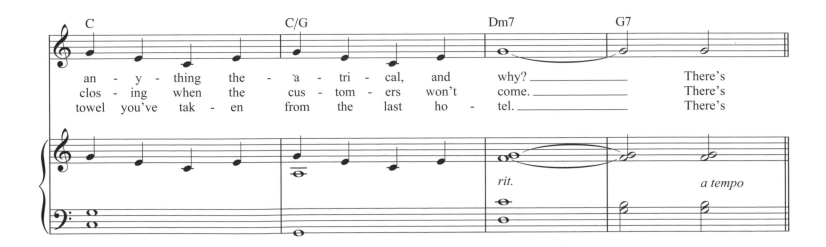

an - y - thing the - a - tri - cal, and why? _____ There's
clos - ing when the cus - tom - ers won't come. _____ There's
towel you've tak - en from the last ho - tel. _____ There's

rit.   *a tempo*

200

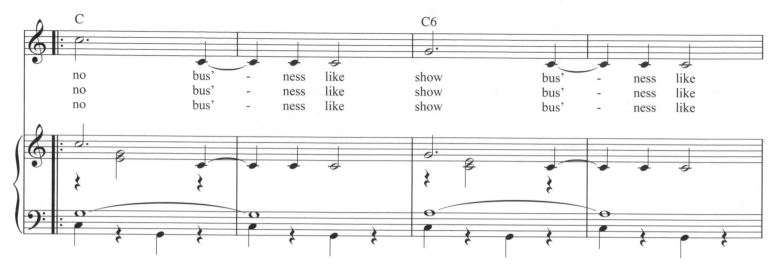

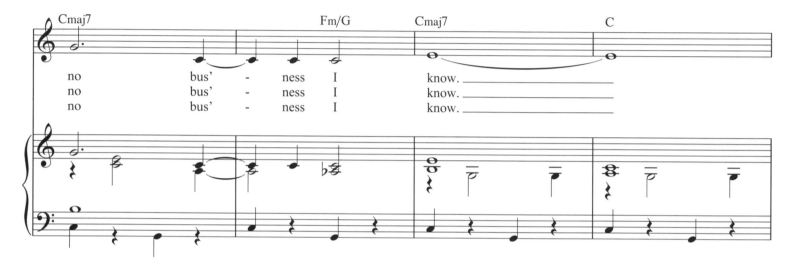

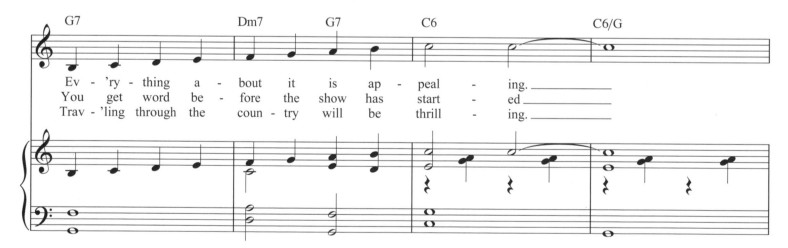

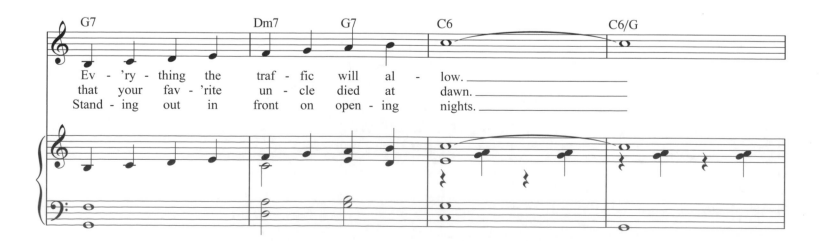

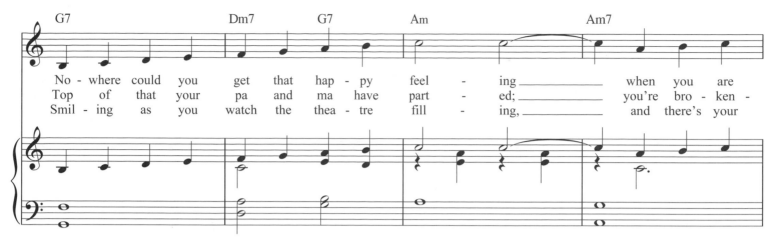

No - where could you get that hap - py feel - ing _____ when you are
Top of that your pa and ma have part - ed; _____ you're bro - ken -
Smil - ing as you watch the thea - tre fill - ing, _____ and there's your

steal - ing _____ that ex - tra bow. _____ There's no peo -
heart - ed, _____ but you go on. _____ There's no peo -
bill - ing _____ out there in lights. _____ There's no peo -

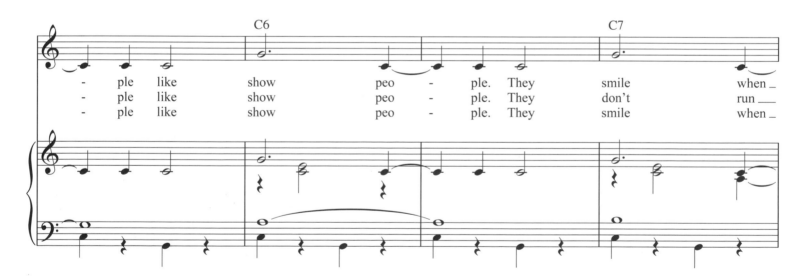

- ple like show peo - ple. They smile when _
- ple like show peo - ple. They don't run _
- ple like show peo - ple. They smile when _

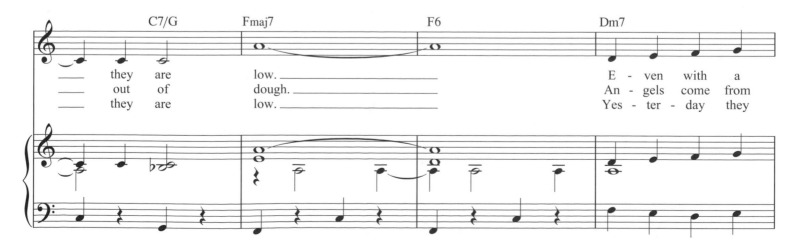

_ they are low. _____ E - ven with a
_ out of dough. _____ An - gels come from
_ they are low. _____ Yes - ter - day they

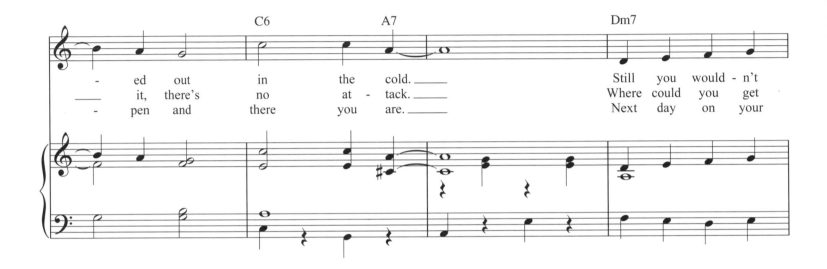

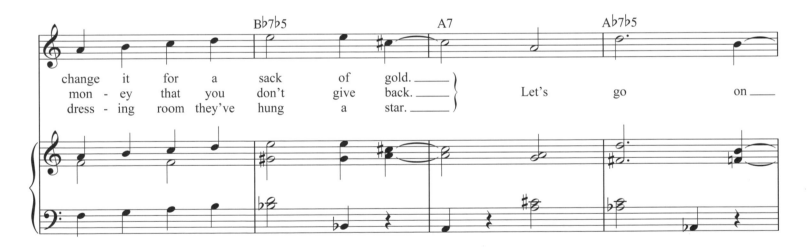

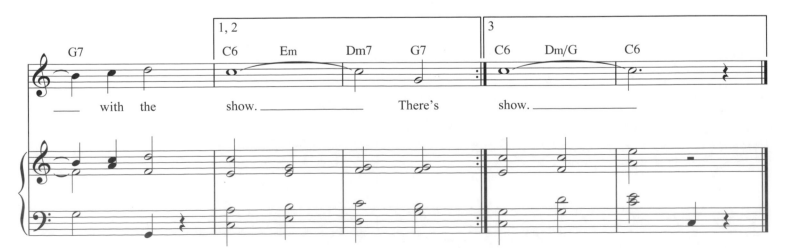

TILL THERE WAS YOU
from Meredith Willson's THE MUSIC MAN

By MEREDITH WILLSON

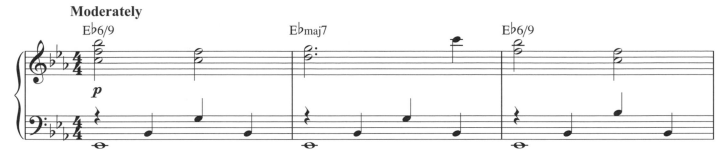

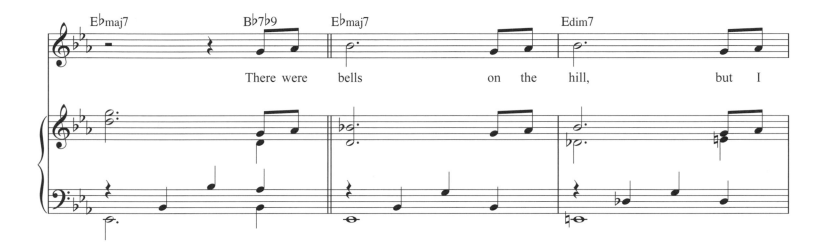

There were bells on the hill, but I

nev-er heard them ring-ing. No, I nev-er heard them at

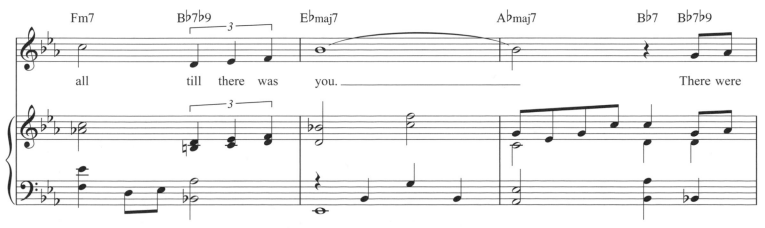

all till there was you. There were

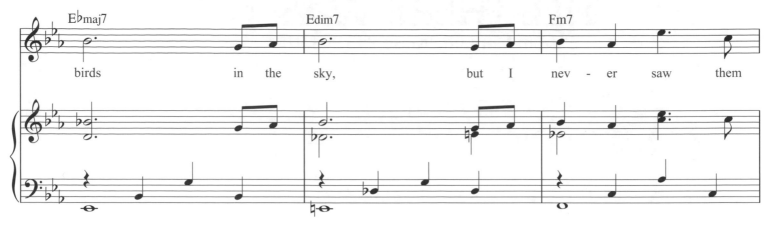

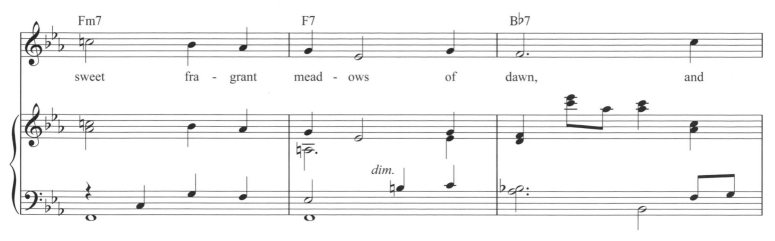

sweet fra - grant mead - ows of dawn, and

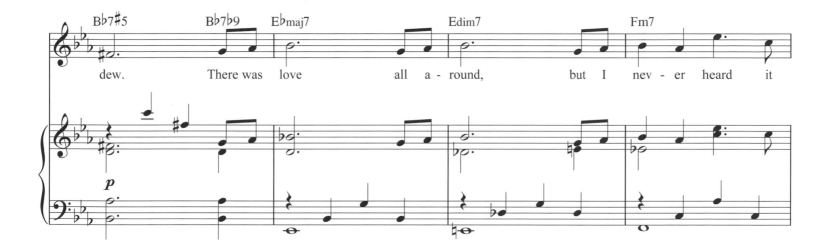

dew. There was love all a - round, but I nev - er heard it

sing - ing.. No, I nev - er heard it at all till there was

you. And there was you. _____

TOMORROW

from the Musical Production ANNIE

Lyric by MARTIN CHARNIN
Music by CHARLES STROUSE

none. When I'm stuck with a day that's grey and

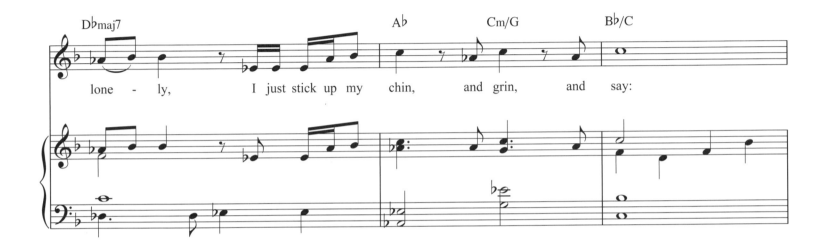

lone - ly, I just stick up my chin, and grin, and say:

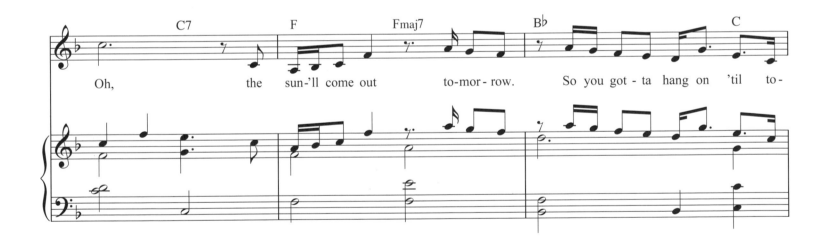

Oh, the sun-'ll come out to-mor-row. So you got-ta hang on 'til to-

mor - row, come what may. To - mor-row, to - mor-row, I

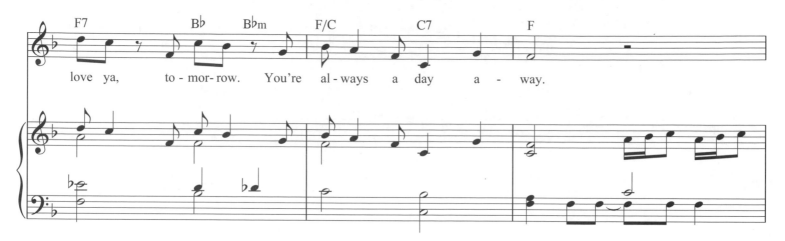

love ya, to-mor-row. You're al-ways a day a-way.

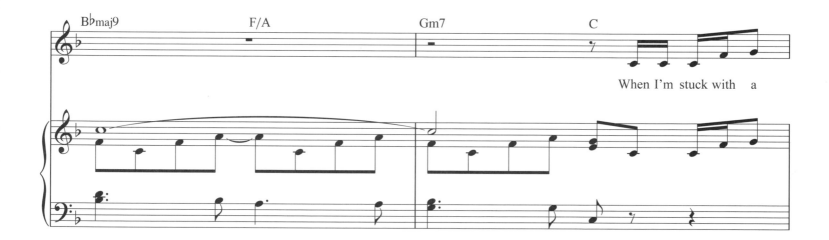

When I'm stuck with a

day that's grey and lone - ly, I just stick up my

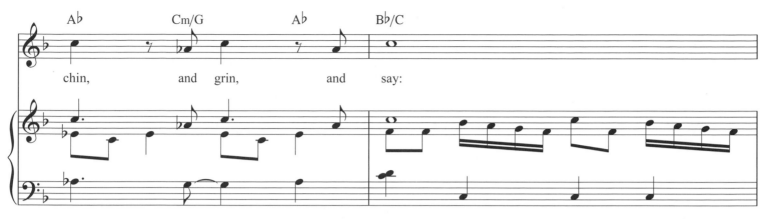

chin, and grin, and say:

Oh, the sun-'ll come out to-mor-row.

So you got-ta hang on 'til to-mor-row, come what may. To-

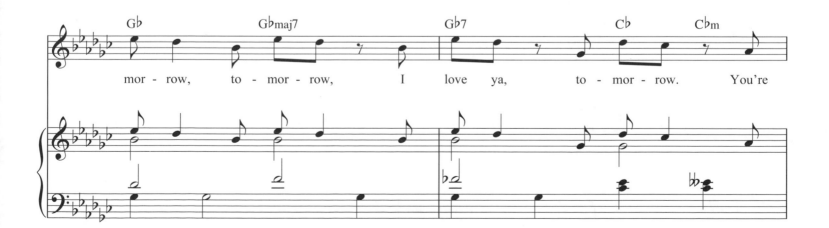

mor-row, to-mor-row, I love ya, to-mor-row. You're

210

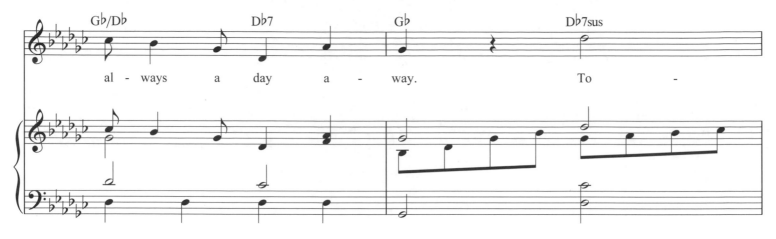

al - ways a day a - way. To -

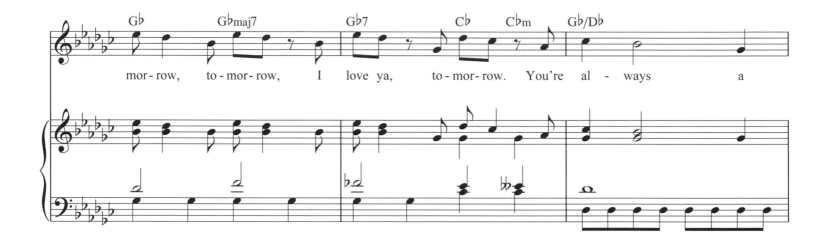

mor - row, to - mor - row, I love ya, to - mor - row. You're al - ways a

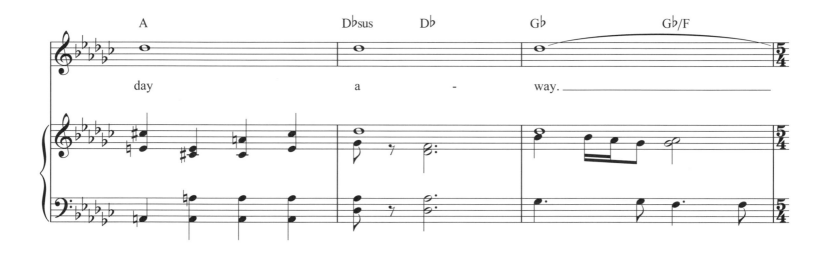

day a - way.

TONIGHT
from WEST SIDE STORY

Lyrics by STEPHEN SONDHEIM
Music by LEONARD BERNSTEIN

212

night, to - night, I'll see my love to -

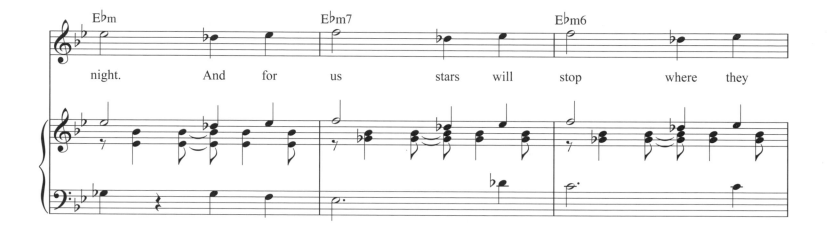

night. And for us stars will stop where they

are! _____ To - day the min - utes seem like

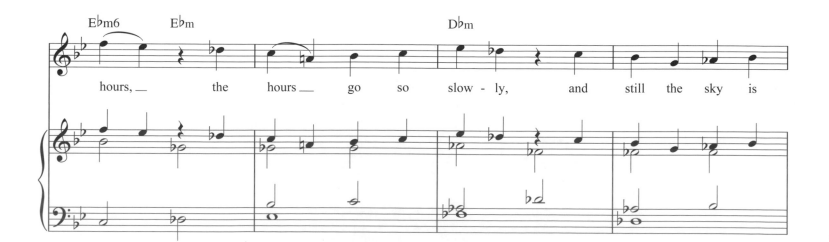

hours, __ the hours __ go so slow - ly, and still the sky is

TRY TO REMEMBER

from THE FANTASTICKS

Words by TOM JONES
Music by HARVEY SCHMIDT

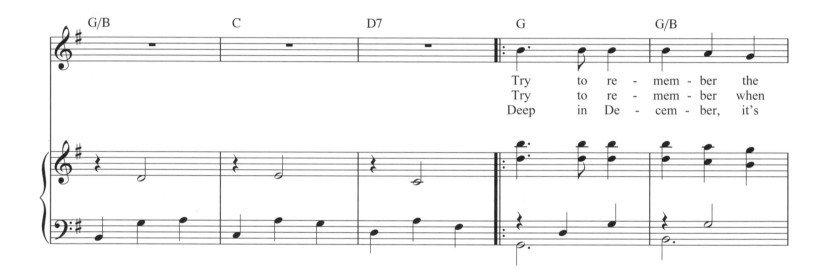

Try to re - mem - ber the
Try to re - mem - ber when
Deep in De - cem - ber, it's

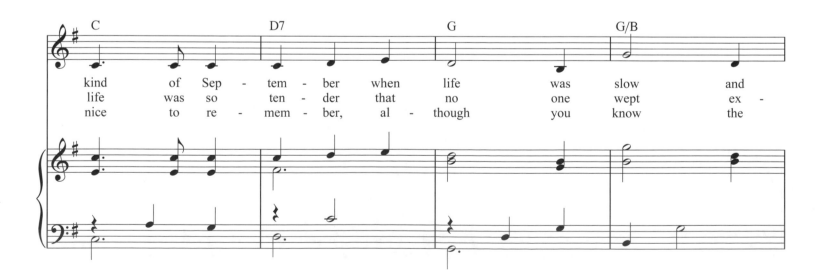

kind of Sep - tem - ber when life was slow and
life was so ten - der that no one wept ex -
nice to re - mem - ber, al - though you know the

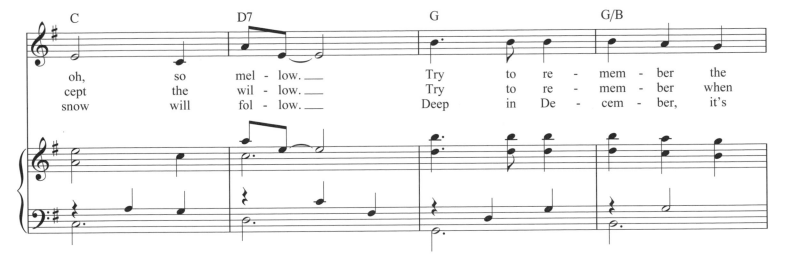

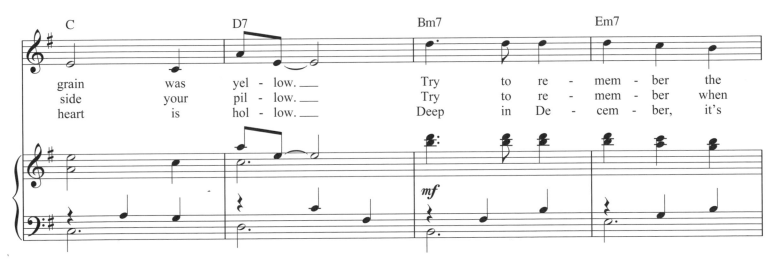

cal - low fel - low. __ Try to re - mem - ber and
bout to bil - low. __ Try to re - mem - ber and
made us mel - low. __ Deep in De - cem - ber, our

if you re - mem - ber, then fol - low. __
if you re - mem - ber, then fol - low. __
hearts should re - mem - ber and

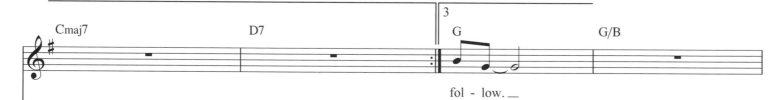

fol - low. __

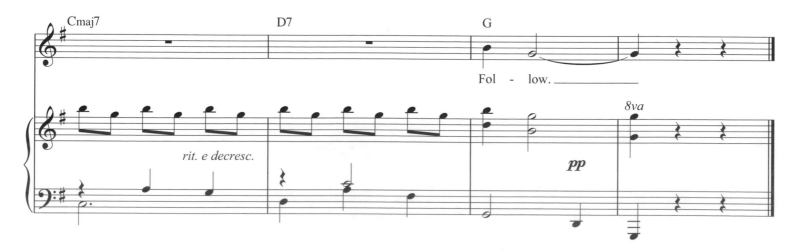

Fol - low. _____

WHERE IS LOVE?

from the Broadway Musical OLIVER!

Words and Music by
LIONEL BART

Slowly, but rhythmically

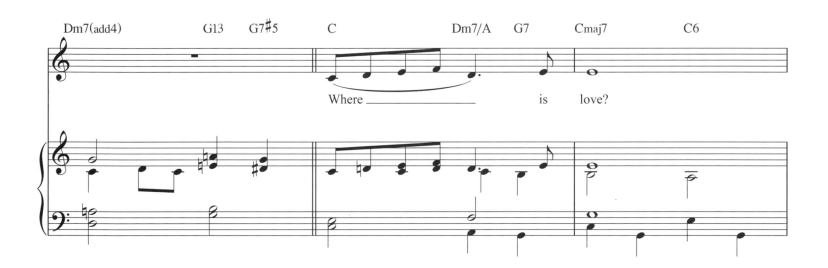

Where _____ is love?

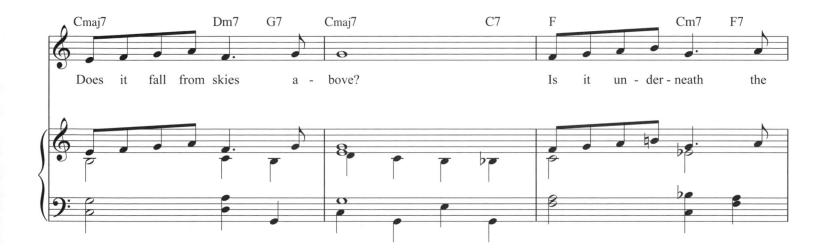

Does it fall from skies a - bove?   Is it un - der - neath the

wil - low tree ___ that I've been dream - ing of?

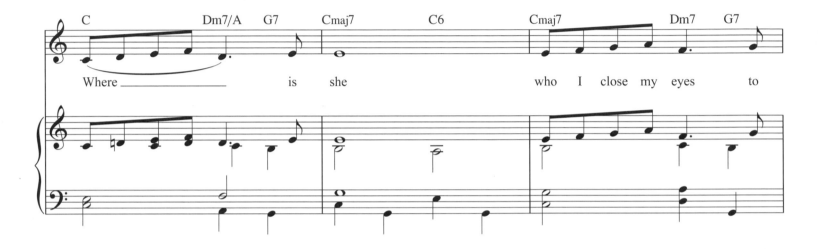

Where ___ is she who I close my eyes to

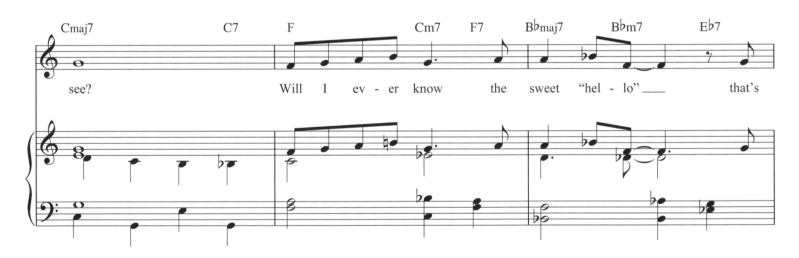

see? Will I ev - er know the sweet "hel - lo" ___ that's

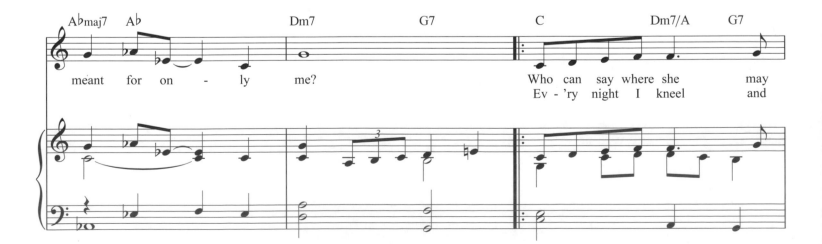

meant for on - ly me? Who can say where she may
Ev - 'ry night I kneel and

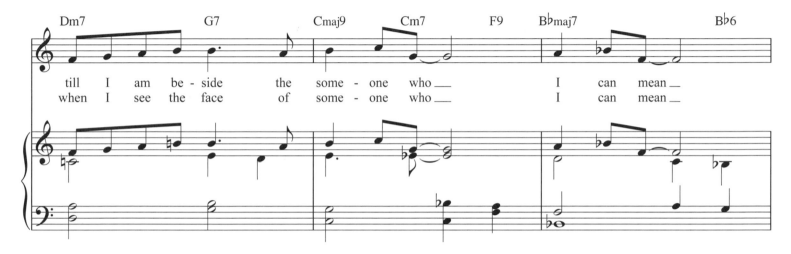

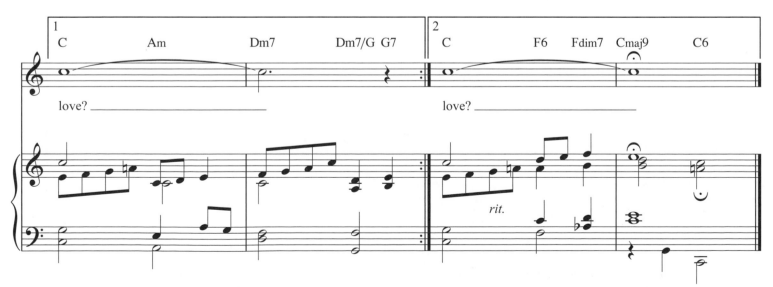

WHAT I DID FOR LOVE

from A CHORUS LINE

Music by MARVIN HAMLISCH
Lyric by EDWARD KLEBAN

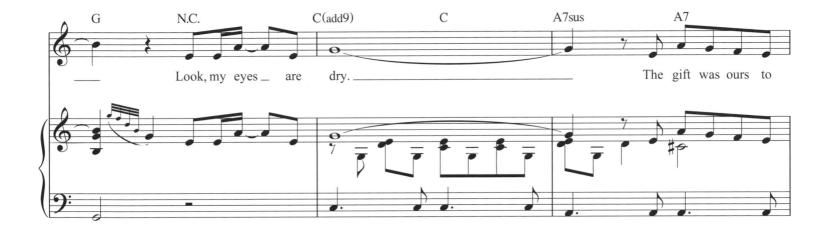

222

what I did for love. _____ Gone, _____

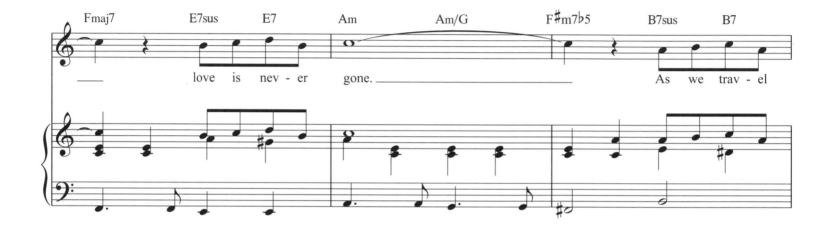

love is nev - er gone. _____ As we trav - el

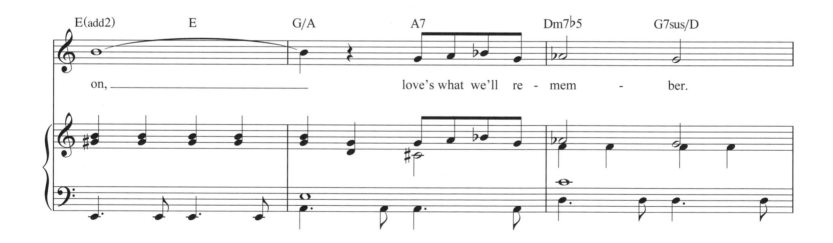

on, _____ love's what we'll re - mem - ber.

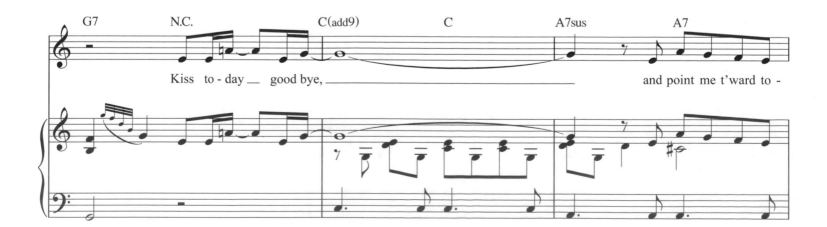

Kiss to - day _ good bye, _____ and point me t'ward to -

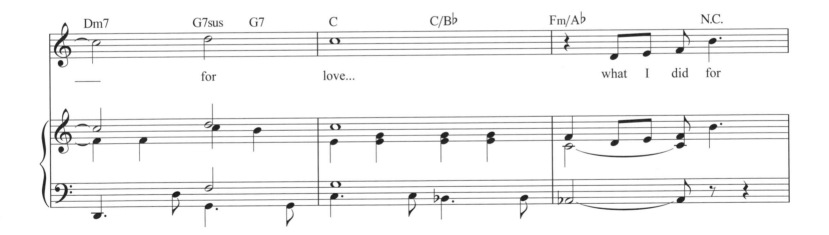

WOULDN'T IT BE LOVERLY

from MY FAIR LADY

Lyrics by ALAN JAY LERNER
Music by FREDERICK LOEWE

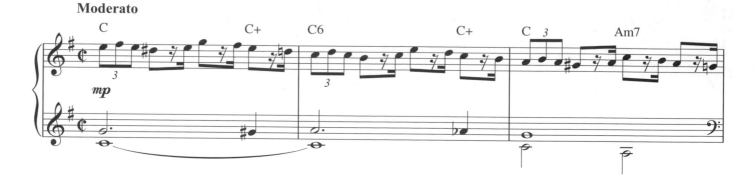

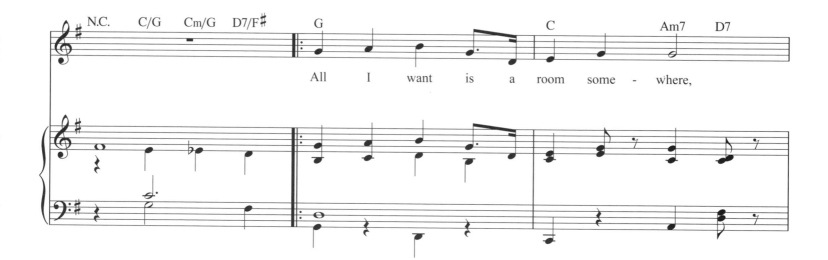

All I want is a room some - where,

Far a - way from the cold night air, With one e-

lov - er - ly sit - tin' ab - so-bloom - in' - lute - ly still!

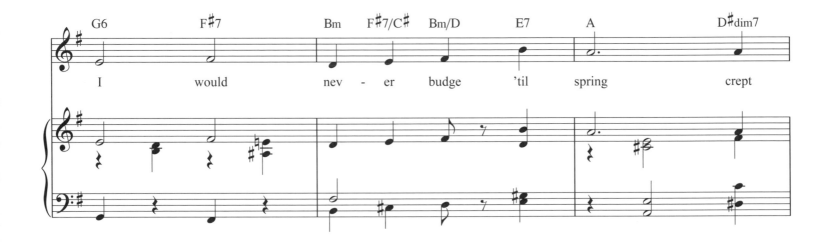

I would nev - er budge 'til spring crept

o - ver the win - dow-sill. Some - one's head rest - in' on my knee,

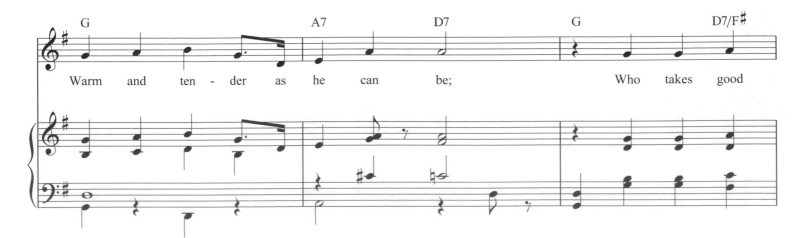

Warm and ten - der as he can be; Who takes good

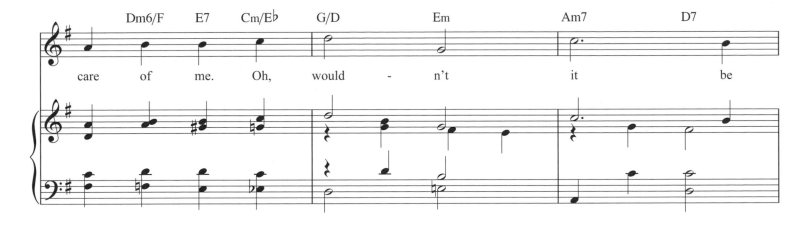

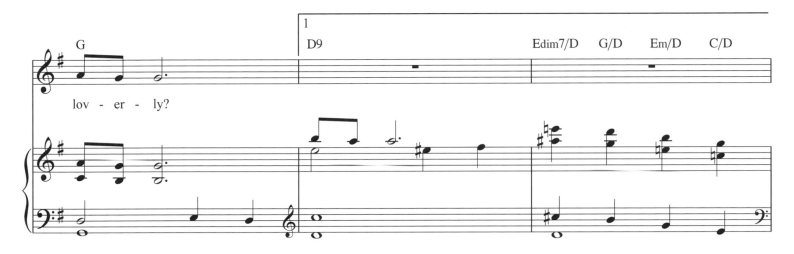

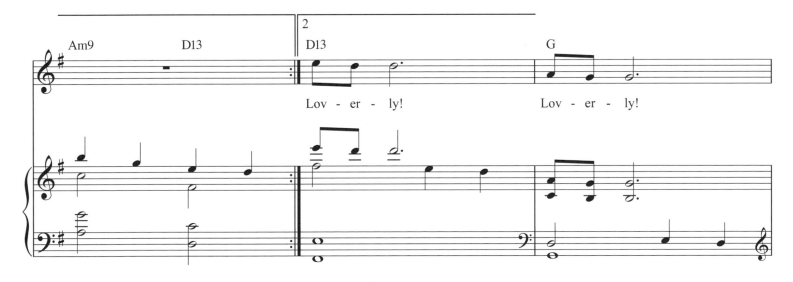

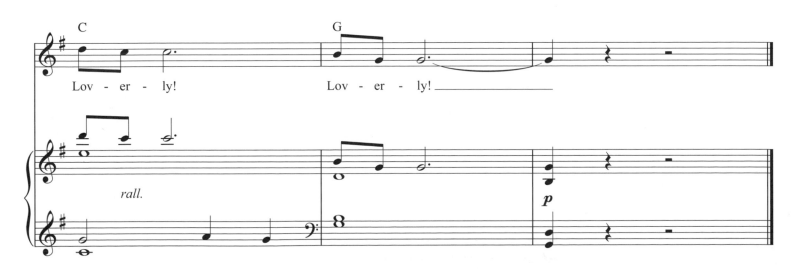

YOU'LL NEVER WALK ALONE

from CAROUSEL

Lyrics by OSCAR HAMMERSTEIN II
Music by RICHARD RODGERS

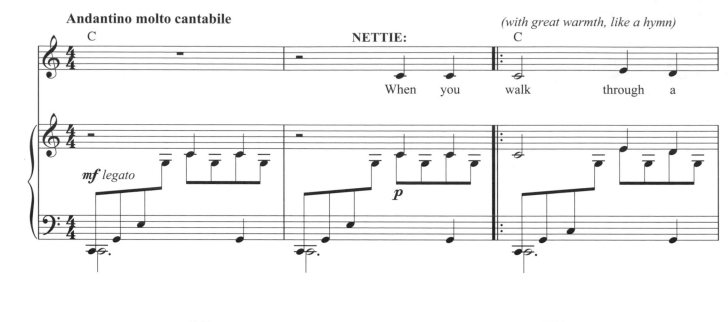

Andantino molto cantabile

NETTIE:

(with great warmth, like a hymn)

When you walk through a

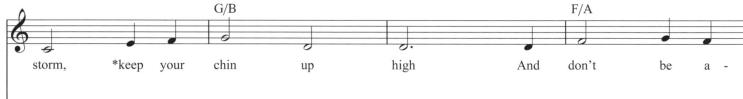

storm, *keep your chin up high And don't be a-

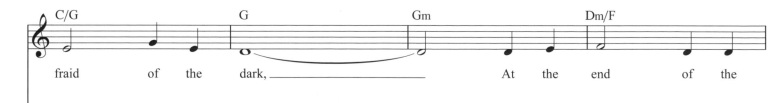

fraid of the dark, _____ At the end of the

* alternate lyric: hold your head up high

229

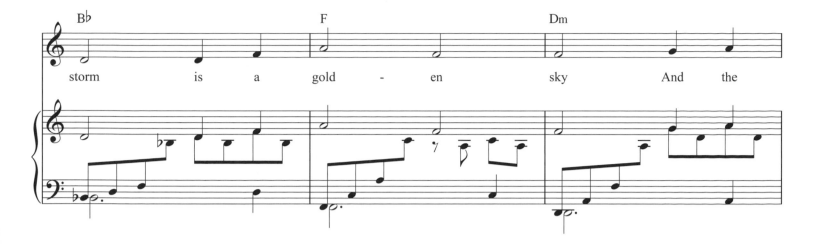

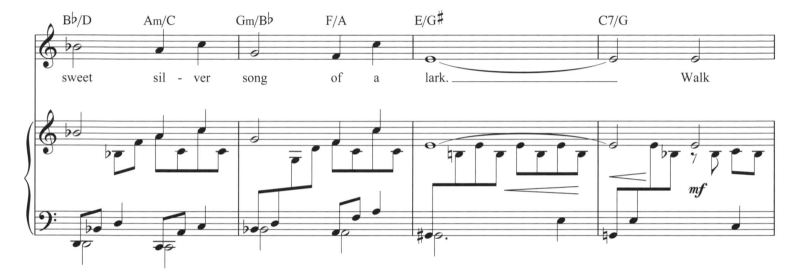

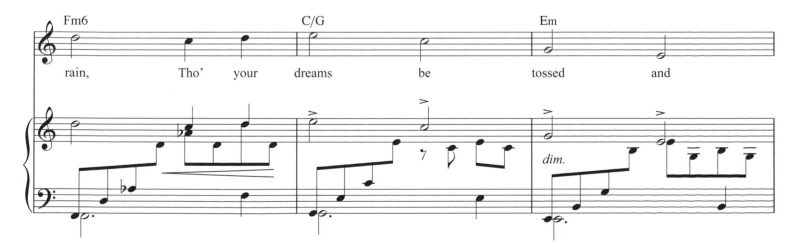

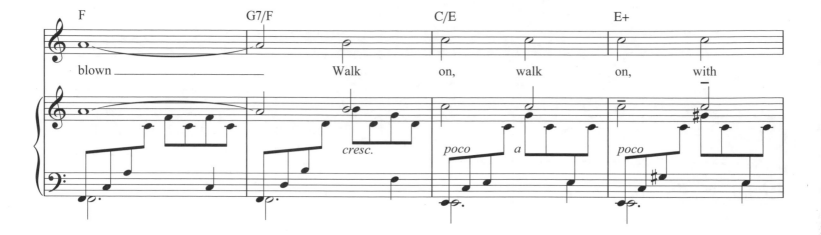

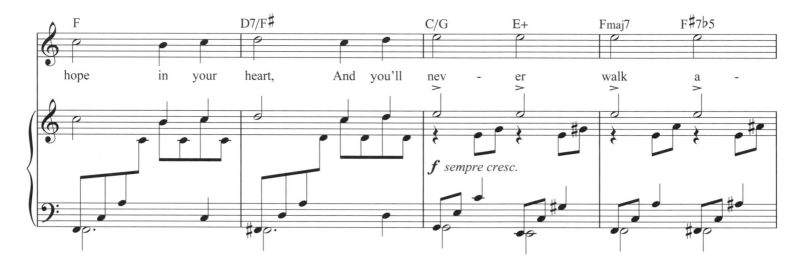

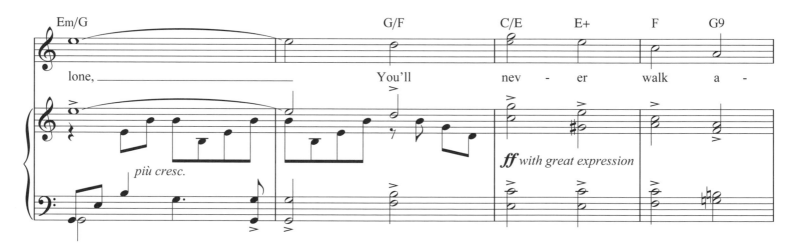

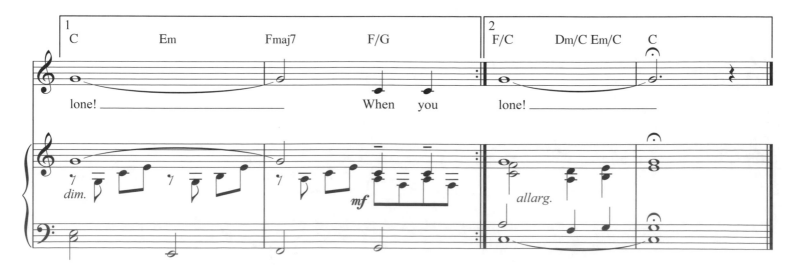

HAL LEONARD:
Your Source for the Best of Broadway

THE BEST BROADWAY SONGS EVER

Over 80 songs from Broadway's latest and greatest hit shows: As Long as He Needs Me • Bess, You Is My Woman • Bewitched • Comedy Tonight • Don't Cry for Me Argentina • Getting to Know You • I Could Have Danced All Night • I Dreamed a Dream • If I Were a Rich Man • The Last Night of the World • Love Changes Everything • Oklahoma • Ol' Man River • People • Try to Remember • and more.
00309155 Piano/Vocal/Guitar $24.99

THE BEST SHOWTUNES EVER

This show-stopping collection features over 70 songs that'll make you want to sing and dance, including: Ain't Misbehavin' • Aquarius • But Not for Me • Day by Day • Defying Gravity • Forty-Second Street • It's De-Lovely • Lullaby of Broadway • On My Own • Over the Rainbow • Send in the Clowns • Singin' in the Rain • Summertime • Whatever Lola Wants (Lola Gets) • and more.
00118782 Piano/Vocal/Guitar $19.99

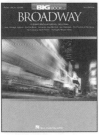

THE BIG BOOK OF BROADWAY

This edition includes 70 songs from classic musicals and recent blockbusters like *The Producers, Aida* and *Hairspray*. Includes: Bring Him Home • Camelot • Everything's Coming Up Roses • The Impossible Dream • A Lot of Livin' to Do • One • Some Enchanted Evening • Thoroughly Modern Millie • Till There Was You • and more.
00311658 Piano/Vocal/Guitar $19.99

BROADWAY CLASSICS
PIANO PLAY-ALONG SERIES, VOLUME 4

This book/CD pack provides keyboardists with a full performance track and a separate backing track for each tune. Songs include: Ain't Misbehavin' • Cabaret • If I Were a Bell • Memory • Oklahoma • Some Enchanted Evening • The Sound of Music • You'll Never Walk Alone.
00311075 Book/CD Pack $14.95

BROADWAY MUSICALS SHOW BY SHOW 2006-2013

31 shows are covered in the latest addition to this unique series, which showcases Broadway's biggest hits year-by-year and show-by-show. A sampling of the shows covered include: Spring Awakening (2006) • In the Heights (2008) • The Addams Family (2010) • The Book of Mormon (2011) • Once (2012) • A Gentleman's Guide to Love and Murder (2013) • and many more.
00123369 Piano/Vocal $19.99

BROADWAY SONGS

Get more bang for your buck with this jam-packed collection of 73 songs from 56 shows, including *Annie Get Your Gun, Cabaret, The Full Monty, Jekyll & Hyde, Les Misérables, Oklahoma* and more. Songs: Any Dream Will Do • Consider Yourself • Footloose • Getting to Know You • I Dreamed a Dream • One • People • Summer Nights • The Surrey with the Fringe on Top • With One Look • and more.
00310832 Piano/Vocal/Guitar $14.99

DEFINITIVE BROADWAY

142 of the greatest show tunes ever, including: Don't Cry for Me Argentina • Hello, Dolly! • I Dreamed a Dream • Lullaby of Broadway • Mack the Knife • Memory • Send in the Clowns • Somewhere • The Sound of Music • Strike Up the Band • Summertime • Sunrise, Sunset • Tea for Two • Tomorrow • What I Did for Love • and more.
00359570 Piano/Vocal/Guitar $24.99

ESSENTIAL SONGS: BROADWAY

Over 100 songs are included in this top-notch collection: Any Dream Will Do • Blue Skies • Cabaret • Don't Cry for Me, Argentina • Edelweiss • Hello, Dolly! • I'll Be Seeing You • Memory • The Music of the Night • Oklahoma • Seasons of Love • Summer Nights • There's No Business like Show Business • Tomorrow • and more.
00311222 Piano/Vocal/Guitar $24.99

FIRST 50 BROADWAY SONGS YOU SHOULD PLAY ON THE PIANO

50 simply arranged, must-know Broadway favorites are featured in this collection of easy piano arrangements. Includes: All I Ask of You • Cabaret • Consider Yourself • Don't Cry for Me Argentina • Edelweiss • Getting to Know You • Hello, Dolly! • I Could Have Danced All Night • I Dreamed a Dream • Memory • Oh, What a Beautiful Mornin' • Ol' Man River • Sunrise, Sunset • Tomorrow • and more.
00150167 Easy Piano $14.99

KIDS' BROADWAY SONGBOOK

An unprecedented collection of songs originally performed by children on the Broadway stage. Includes 16 songs for boys and girls, including: Gary, Indiana (*The Music Man*) • Castle on a Cloud (*Les Misérables*) • Where Is Love? (*Oliver!*) • Tomorrow (*Annie*) • and more.
00311609 Book Only $16.99
00740149 Book/Online Audio $24.99

THE OFF-BROADWAY SONGBOOK

42 gems from off-Broadway hits, including *Godspell, Tick Tick... Boom!, The Fantasticks, Once upon a Mattress, The Wild Party* and more. Songs include: Always a Bridesmaid • Come to Your Senses • Day by Day • Happiness • How Glory Goes • I Hate Musicals • The Picture in the Hall • Soon It's Gonna Rain • Stars and the Moon • Still Hurting • Twilight • and more.
00311168 Piano/Vocal/Guitar $19.99

THE TONY AWARDS SONGBOOK

This collection assembles songs from each of Tony-winning Best Musicals through "Mama Who Bore Me" from 2007 winner *Spring Awakening*. Songs include: Til There Was You • The Sound of Music • Hello, Dolly! • Sunrise, Sunset • Send in the Clowns • Tomorrow • Memory • I Dreamed a Dream • Seasons of Love • Circle of Life • Mama, I'm a Big Girl Now • and more. Includes photos and a table of contents listed both chronologically and alphabetically.
00311092 Piano/Vocal/Guitar $19.95

THE ULTIMATE BROADWAY FAKE BOOK

Over 700 songs from more than 200 Broadway shows! Songs include: All I Ask of You • Bewitched • Cabaret • Don't Cry for Me Argentina • Edelweiss • Getting to Know You • Hello, Dolly! • If I Were a Rich Man • Last Night of the World • The Music of the Night • Oklahoma • People • Seasons of Love • Tell Me on a Sunday • Unexpected Song • and more!
00240046 Melody/Lyrics/Chords $49.99

Prices, contents, and availability subject to change without notice.
Some products may not be available outside the U.S.A.

Get complete songlists and more at www.halleonard.com

1216